CREATIVE
BIBLE LESSONS
IN

Revelation

12 Futuristic Sessions on Never-Ending Worship

RANDY SOUTHERN

ZONDERVAN™

WWW.ZONDERVAN.COM

D1532769

Youth Specialties

www.YouthSpecialties.com

Creative Bible Lessons in Revelation: 12 Futuristic Sessions on Never-Ending Worship

Copyright © 2003 by Youth Specialties

Youth Specialties Books, 300 South Pierce Street, El Cajon, CA 92020, are published by Zondervan, 5300 Patterson Aveune SE, Grand Rapids, MI 49530

Library of Congress Cataloging-in-Publication Data

Southern, Randy.
  Creative Bible lessons in Revelation : 12 futuristic sessions on
never-ending worship / by Randy Southern.
        p. cm.
  ISBN 0-310-25108-7 (pbk.)
  1. Bible. N.T. Revelation--Study and teaching. 2. Christian education
of teenagers. I. Title.
  BS2825.55.S67 2003
  228'.0071--dc21

                                                                    2003004625

Edited by Tamara Rice

Cover design by Jack Rogers

Interior design by Brian Smith

Printed in the United States of America

  04 05 06 07 08 09 / / 10 9 8 7 6 5 4 3

Dedication:

To my wife, Ann, for her faith, strength, courage, and love in the face of an uncertain future.

- R.S.

CREATIVE BIBLE LESSONS IN REVELATION

CONTENTS

You Say You Want a Revelation...

For many Christians the book of Revelation is the "crazy uncle" in the New Testament family—we know we should treat him with the same respect we do the other relatives, but we can't. He's just so different from the others. In fact he's a little weird—and even a little scary.

The problem is most of the time, we have no idea what he's talking about. His words make no sense to us. Whenever interaction with him is unavoidable, we try to make the best of it—but we take the first opportunity we can find to split to find safer, more familiar faces to spend our time with, like James or Peter or John.

The problem with the "crazy uncle" approach to Revelation is he actually has a lot to say—deep stuff, interesting stuff, life-changing stuff. If you were to ignore him, it might be at your own peril.

For example the book of Revelation contains some of the most inspirational—and educational—passages on the topic of **worship** in all of Scripture. The heavenly style of praise and adoration described in Revelation should serve as a model for our worship here on earth. Without a working knowledge of the book of Revelation then, we can't fulfil one of our primary responsibilities as Christians—that of worship—in the way God intends.

The Matter of Prefixes

The question that inevitably arises in any study of Revelation is interpretation. Does this book promote—

- amillennialism?
- postmillennialism?
- pretribulational premillennialism?
- midtribulational premillenialism?
- posttribulational premillennialism?
- new-and-improved premillennialism with fluoride and an active whitening agent?

If you're scanning the page for words or phrases revealing the eschatological leanings of this book, don't bother. Eschatology isn't what the material is about. So if you're looking for a study of Revelation containing...

- capsulated biographies of the originators of premillennialism
- explorations of the sociopolitical landscape of first-century Rome
- 37 possible candidates for antichristhood

...then good luck in your continued search.

If, however, you're looking for a study addressing the mysterious, apocalyptic nature of Revelation while at the same time promoting practical application of the principles found within, this is the study for you!

What's in It?

The material in *Creative Bible Lessons in Revelation* is organized for maximum efficiency.

- **Sound Bite** provides an overview of the session topic in one or two sentences.
- **Kickoff** offers two different ideas for opening activities and games to introduce the session topic.
- **Focusing In** brings clarity to the session topic using carefully chosen exercises and questions.
- **Hitting the Book** offers thought-provoking Bible study questions that work equally well for individuals and small groups.
- **Making It Count** provides helpful application exercises—ways for students to put the principles of Revelation to use in their everyday lives.

NOTES: In the "You'll need" box at the start of each lesson, you might see things like "TV" and "DVD player" listed as necessary items. But go ahead and use a VCR if the DVD players are scarce. If you have access to a video-projection unit, go for it. If it's more convenient to use an overhead projector and transparencies or a flip chart and markers, please do. You won't see all the variations in these lists of materials you need, but you should substitute whatever works for you, your budget, and the size of your group! (Please be sure to screen all clips before you play them for the group. If language is a problem in key scenes, turn down the volume or—if you have the time and equipment—edit it out).

And don't forget you can download all the repro pages for free: www.YouthSpecialties.com/store/downloads (password: **rev**).

For those who want to go the extra mile, look for these tidbits—

- **More More More** offers occasional supplements to the activities and discussions.
- **Let's Get Theological** offers guidance for introducing students to various Christian schools of thought regarding the events described in Revelation.
- **Worthy of Worship** offers suggestions for turning ordinary youth meetings into extraordinary times of praising God.

Finally...

May God richly bless you as you open your students' eyes to the awesome wonders lying within the last book of his Word. May his Holy Spirit guide you as you attempt to help them make peace with the crazy uncle of the New Testament family.

1

What Lies Beyond
Revelation 1

We may not know exactly what the future holds, but we know who holds the future.

What You'll Need

- Bibles
- Pens
- Index cards (optional)
- TV and DVD player (optional)
- Movies with futuristic themes (optional)
- Magic 8-Ball
- Whiteboard and markers
- Copies of **A Letter from John** (pages 16-17), one for each student
- Copies of **You're in Good Hands** (page 18), one for each student

I Predict

This activity will work especially well if you have a small group whose members are familiar with each other. Before the session, hand out index cards and ask students to write down four predictions of things they think will happen during the meeting. Emphasize that the predictions must be specific in order to be counted.

Specific, acceptable predictions might include things like—

- Abdul will make Mallory laugh.
- Lindsay will ask if we can play volleyball tonight.
- Carlos will begin his prayer by saying, "Our gracious heavenly Father."

Vague, unacceptable predictions might include things like—

- People will stand up after the meeting.
- We will play a game tonight.
- Someone will pray sometime during the meeting.

If a student's prediction comes true during the meeting, she should say, "I called it!" loud enough for everyone to hear. After you verify the prediction, reward the "prophet" with a piece of gum or candy. Do the same for anyone else whose predictions come true.

Segue into the session topic using questions like—

YOUTH WORKER SCRIPT

- **Without telling us your predictions, what did you base them on?**
- **If you were to make a prediction about the distant future, what would it be?**
- **When you think about what the future is going to be like, what do you base your impressions on?**

NOTE: This activity—and the one that follows, involving a Magic 8-Ball—isn't meant to endorse divination or any other unbiblical practice. Quite the contrary! You'll find at the conclusion of the Magic 8-Ball activity that you're encouraged to clue your students into the fact that human attempts to figure everything out are futile—and that God has all the answers we'll ever need.

Clips Ahoy

Show several brief video clips from films either set in the future or depicting the future. (Be sure to screen each clip for objectionable material before you show it to your students.) Among the movie titles you might consider for these clips are—

12 Monkeys	Sleeper
2001: A Space Odyssey	Soylent Green
A.I.—Artificial Intelligence	Star Trek
Blade Runner	Star Wars
The Fifth Element	THX 1138
The Matrix	The Terminator
Minority Report	The Time Machine
Planet of the Apes	Total Recall

Find a scene in each film illustrating its depiction of the future. For example in *The Time Machine*, you might show the scene in which the time traveler wakes up hundreds of thousands of years in the future in the seemingly peaceful, post-technological society of the Eloi.

After your mini film fest, segue into the lesson with questions like—

YOUTH WORKER SCRIPT

- Which, if any, of these visions of the future do you think will turn out to be most accurate?
- What do you think the world will be like 100 years from now? How about 500 years from now? How about 1,000 years from now?
- Will the world get better or worse in the future? What makes you think so?

If you get vague responses, encourage your students to think about specific aspects of the future, such as medical technology, transportation, climate conditions, crime, or fashion.

Focusing In

Once Upon the Future

Pass around a Magic 8-Ball and let students take turns asking it questions about the future ("Will we beat Central this weekend?" "Will I pass my English midterm?" "Will this youth group meeting turn out to be the best time I've ever had in my life?") and then revealing its answers to the group. Then ask—

YOUTH WORKER SCRIPT

What are some other things people do to try to figure out what's going to happen in the future?

If no one else mentions it, point out that some people have tealeaves or tarot cards read for them by so-called psychics. Others have their palms or the bumps on their heads read. Others rely on horoscopes and astrology, and still others look for clues about the future in their dreams.

Emphasize that contrary to the claims of countless psychic hotline commercials, there's only one guaranteed revelation of the future. Lest any of your students miss the point, hold up a Bible.

Use any or all of the following questions to gauge your students' knowledge and opinion of the book of Revelation:

- How many of you have ever studied the book of Revelation before? What did you think of it? What advice would you give to someone who was just beginning to study it?
- How many of you have ever tried to just read the book of Revelation? How would you describe the book?
- If someone were to ask you what the book of Revelation was about, what would you tell them?

Record students' answers on a flip chart or whiteboard. If any of your students are fans of the *Left Behind* series, be prepared to explain the difference between the events portrayed in those books (in other words the creative license taken by the authors) and the events actually described in the book of Revelation.

If you find your students don't have a lot of previous experience with or opinions about the book of Revelation, give them a minute or so to get a taste of it. Distribute Bibles and instruct them to search Revelation as fast as they can to find one verse they can understand and one verse that makes absolutely no sense to them. Ask a couple of volunteers to share their discoveries. Briefly discuss some of the strange images and passages your students find.

Afterward introduce the next section by saying something like—

If Revelation seems like a strange book to you, join the club. Scholars and theologians have been arguing for centuries about what the book actually means and what it tells us about the future. The reason for the debate becomes obvious when you take a look at how the apostle John wrote the book.

Some parts of Revelation read like a science fiction novel. Other parts read like a script for a disaster movie. Still other parts read like a hymnal. Very few parts are done in a straightforward way, which leaves it open to a lot of interpretation.

The good news is we don't have to know exactly what each image in the book represents or what each prophecy means in order to discover some life-changing facts about our future.

Hitting the Book

A Letter from John

Distribute pens and copies of **A Letter from John** (pages 16-17) to your students while they're in the large group…then let 'em work in small groups to complete the sheet. Also, please gauge how much time you think this worksheet will take your group—feel free to highlight only key questions while eliminating others. Now…you may want to use the following comments in your discussion of Revelation 1:

YOUTH WORKER SCRIPT

- The fact that the book of Revelation is the Word of God means it's entirely truthful. We may not be able to understand everything in it, but we know God will accomplish everything he says he will do.

- The fact that Revelation is God's Word also means its every bit as deserving of our attention as the seemingly easy books of the Bible. In other words we can't shrug off Revelation as being too hard to understand and leave it at that. We have a responsibility to study and understand it to the best of our ability.

- Though the book is addressed to "the seven churches in the province of Asia"— and no doubt deals with some specific problems they were facing or would face—its truths also apply to the lives of believers today.

- The book of Revelation isn't intended to answer every question we have about the future—it's merely a sneak preview of what lies ahead.

- Despite the disturbing nature of some images and descriptions in Revelation, the book is intended to provide comfort and assurance for believers. Ultimately the future lies in the hands of our heavenly Father.

You're in Good Hands

Distribute copies of **You're in Good Hands** (page 18). Give students a few minutes to complete the top half of the sheet, then ask volunteers to share which events they rated highest and why. Then you might say something like—

YOUTH WORKER SCRIPT

The reason God is able to reveal the future to us in his Word is he's all-knowing. He knows exactly when every future event is going to happen and what the results will be. On a personal level, he knows every decision we will ever face, as well as every possible outcome. On top of that, God is all-powerful. Nothing is beyond his control—not even future events. Nothing can happen if he doesn't allow it.

The icing on the cake, though, is that God loves, protects, and takes care of us in ways we can't possibly imagine. Don't take my word for it though. See for yourself.

Ask new volunteers to read the following verses:

- *Joshua 1:5b* "I will never leave you nor forsake you."
- *Matthew 11:28* "Come to me, all you who are weary and burdened, and I will give you rest."
- *1 Peter 5:7* "Cast all your anxiety on him because he cares for you."

Then continue with something like—

YOUTH WORKER SCRIPT

God—the one who holds the future—invites us to give him our fears and worries about the future and let him take care of them. That's a great offer—especially when you consider he's the only one who can do something about them!

Instruct students to look back at **You're in Good Hands** and choose one item from the list of future concerns—the one they rated as causing them the most anxiety—and really place it in God's hands by writing it in the picture on the bottom half of the sheet. Wrap up the session by asking volunteers to share briefly what it means to place a concern in God's hands and how it should affect our feelings about it.

MORE MORE MORE

You're in Good Hands

Ask your students how they feel about the future. Rather than having them answer with their mouths though, let them do it with their feet.

Set up an imaginary continuum in your meeting area. Announce that one wall represents *Complete Excitement and Eagerness* while the wall on the other side of the room represents *Complete Fear and Dread*. Ask students to stand in a place on the continuum representing their true feelings. Ask several students, especially those at each end, to explain their responses.

A Letter From John

Read the Scripture passages indicated, then answer the questions that follow. (This isn't a test—you can look back at the verses whenever you need to!)

Revelation 1:1-3

1. What did God do to let John know the vision he was about to see was no ordinary daydream?

2. What does it mean to us that the words in the book of Revelation are actually the words of God?

3. How might a person be blessed by reading the book of Revelation?

4. Give an example of how a person might take to heart what is written in it.

5. What goes through your mind when you see a phrase like "the time is near" in verse 3?

Revelation 1:4-8

6. When Revelation was written it was a bad time to be a Christian. The Romans believed their emperor was Lord and were persecuting those who believed otherwise. Many Christians were being tortured and killed because of their faith. Believers who

met together in churches did so at their own risk. Describe what it must have been like to be one of the people in the seven churches mentioned in verse 4.

7. How do you suppose the seven churches felt about receiving a letter from one of Jesus' closest friends?

8. Why do you suppose John was so quick to mention Jesus' return in verse 7?

9. How do you think the believers of John's day felt about the idea of Jesus coming back?

Revelation 1:9-20

10. John was the only one of Jesus' 11 faithful disciples who wasn't executed because of his beliefs. Instead he was banished to the island of Patmos. Based on his experience what kind of "patient endurance" do you think he was talking about in verse 9?

11. Why is patient endurance still important for believers today?

12. Why do you think God gave John—and all believers—glimpses of the future?

You're in Good Hands

Rate each of the following future events on a scale of 1 to 10, based on how much anxiety or concern it's caused you. (With 1 meaning it's never crossed your mind and 10 meaning you're a nervous wreck about it.)

_____ Finding a boyfriend or girlfriend

_____ Graduating from high school

_____ Getting into the right college

_____ Choosing the right major

_____ Paying for college

_____ Leaving home

_____ Leaving my friends

_____ Getting a good job

_____ Finding a spouse

_____ Losing a loved one

_____ Getting old

_____ Dying

2

The New-Look Jesus
Revelation 1; 5; 19

SOUND BITE

People who picture Jesus as nothing more than a meek and mild teacher may be shocked to see him as the glorified king who returns to earth for the final showdown between good and evil.

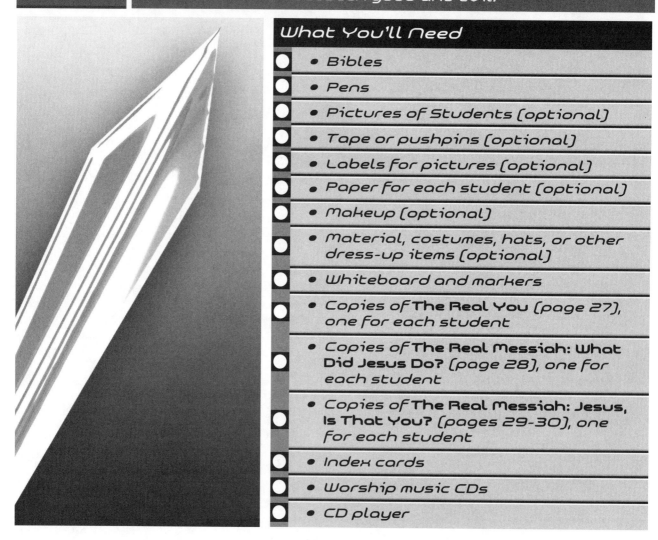

What You'll Need

- Bibles
- Pens
- Pictures of Students (optional)
- Tape or pushpins (optional)
- Labels for pictures (optional)
- Paper for each student (optional)
- Makeup (optional)
- Material, costumes, hats, or other dress-up items (optional)
- Whiteboard and markers
- Copies of **The Real You** (page 27), one for each student
- Copies of **The Real Messiah: What Did Jesus Do?** (page 28), one for each student
- Copies of **The Real Messiah: Jesus, Is That You?** (pages 29-30), one for each student
- Index cards
- Worship music CDs
- CD player

Kickoff Option 1

Unrecognizable—That's What You Are

Contact several of your students before the meeting and ask them to bring pictures of themselves in which they aren't immediately recognizable. Baby pictures would work well, especially if the person has changed quite a bit since infancy. Pictures of students in Halloween costumes or with certain physical features obscured would also work. If you have some shutterbugs in your group, you might encourage them to take their own creatively obscured photos for the activity.

Collect the photos and display them around the room—using pushpins or tape—with an identifying number labelling each one. Give your students paper and pens or pencils and a few minutes to peruse the collection and write down their guesses as to who's who in each picture.

After the guessing is done, segue into your lesson using questions like—

YOUTH WORKER SCRIPT

- Would someone who hasn't seen you in 10 years recognize you today? Why or why not?
- Will we all be able to recognize each other 10 years from now? How about 50 years from now?
- Do you think you would recognize Jesus if he returned today? Why or why not?

Kickoff Option 2

Makeover

Divide the group into teams of four. Explain that one person on each team will be the model and the other three will be makeup artists. The goal is for the artists to make the model as unrecognizable as possible. Give each team a supply of makeup and material or clothes for costumes. When time is up ask each model to parade in front of the group and have students vote on who's least recognizable.

Use questions like these to introduce the lesson:

- Have you ever run into someone who knew you, but who you didn't recognize right away? If so, describe what happened. Why was the person so unrecognizable to you?

- Have you ever run into someone you knew, but the person didn't recognize you right away? If so, describe what happened. Why were you so unrecognizable?

- If you were looking for Jesus in a crowd, do you think you'd be able to recognize him? If so, what would you look for? If not, why not?

Focusing In

The Real You

Distribute pencils and copies of **The Real You** (page 27). After a few minutes, ask volunteers to share their responses. Keep track of the volunteers' answers on a flip chart or whiteboard so you can refer back to them easily. Use any or all of the following questions to guide your discussion of the sheet:

YOUTH WORKER SCRIPT

- How do you explain the fact that people have such different views and opinions about what you're like?
- Who knows you best? Why?
- If someone were to wonder what you're really like, how would you recommend they find out?
- Name something people who don't know you well would be surprised to learn about you.
- Do a lot of people have wrong impressions about what you're like? Why or why not?
- Do you have a lot of wrong opinions about what other people are like? Why or why not?

If no one else mentions it, point out that sometimes we withhold certain parts of our personalities from people in an effort to make them think we're something we're not. In other cases, people may not be able to shake their first impressions of us, no matter how inaccurate those impressions are. Some people base their opinions of us on what other people tell them, instead of finding out for themselves what we're like. If your students are shy, you might get the ball rolling by sharing a little-known fact about yourself—the more surprising, the better. Your willingness to be open and vulnerable with the group will likely go a long way toward encouraging your students to do the same.

MORE MORE MORE

The Real You

You can make a game of the *Real You* activity, but you—or a couple of your students—will need to do some investigative reporting first. Choose three or four students to investigate. Conduct brief interviews for each student—on video if possible—with casual acquaintances, close friends, siblings, and parents. Ask representatives from each group to give you three descriptions of the student in question. Once you've got your answers—either on paper or on video—you can have your featured students try to guess what people said about them.

Hitting the Book

The Real Messiah

Distribute pens and copies of **The Real Messiah: What Did Jesus Do?** (page 28) to your students while they're in the large group…then let 'em work in small groups to complete the sheet. Also, please gauge how much time you think this worksheet will take your group—feel free to highlight only key questions while eliminating others.

If you think students might be self-conscious about their lack of knowledge about Jesus, let them work in pairs to complete the sheet. When they're finished, reveal the answers: *1-a; 2-b; 3-a; 4-d; 5-a.* Ask your students what their impression might be of Jesus if all they knew of him were the five things on the worksheet. Supplement your students' responses as needed by pointing out that Jesus seems passive, meek, and perhaps even a little weak in the situations mentioned on the sheet. Then ask questions like—

- Is this an accurate portrayal of Jesus? Why or why not?
- What are some other wrong impressions people have about Jesus?
- Is there anything harmful or wrong about having an incomplete view of what Jesus is like? Explain your answer.

If no one else mentions it, point out that the Jesus portrayed in the quiz (and often in the media)—the sensitive, nonaggressive teacher and philosopher—is someone we would certainly respect and admire, but not necessarily someone we would worship.

Distribute copies of **The Real Messiah: Jesus, Is That You?** (pages 29-30). Let your students work in small groups to complete the sheet. You may want to use the following comments to supplement your discussion of Revelation 1, 5, and 19:

YOUTH WORKER SCRIPT

- Too often Jesus is written off as a meek, mild philosopher-teacher who went around spreading joy, happiness, and healing with his message of love and non-violence—like some new age guru or something. While there are certainly elements of truth in that portrayal, it doesn't even scratch the surface of who Jesus is and what he's really like.
- When Jesus comes back, it will be as the conquering king. His power and vengeance will be so great that no one and nothing will be able to oppose him.
- The witnesses in heaven described in Revelation 5 offer the only logical reaction to Jesus: they bow down and worship him with everything they have.

The Real Messiah

If you don't have time for **The Real Messiah: What Did Jesus Do?** worksheet, try having your students share their opinions about what certain celebrities are really like. Call out a name and wait for your students to respond. Your list of celebrities might include popular actors, athletes, musicians, the president of the United States, or even your pastor. The last name on your list should be Jesus Christ.

Making It Count

For Better or Worship

Get students thinking about their own motivation for worship, using questions like—

YOUTH WORKER SCRIPT

- **Have you ever had a reaction to Jesus similar to the one the witnesses in heaven in Revelation 5 had—one where you were just overwhelmed by your feelings for him?** (*If you've had a similar experience, share it with the group. Then ask volunteers to do the same.*)
- **What does worship mean to you?**
- **What's the perfect attitude to have during worship?**
- **What are some obstacles that can get in the way of true worship?**
- **What can we do to avoid or overcome those obstacles?**

Distribute index cards and pens or pencils. Ask students to write down three reasons Jesus deserves their worship. Ask them not to settle for typical Sunday school answers—like "He is good." Instead encourage them to think in terms of their personal lives—like "He's given me the strength to overcome some harmful habits." For a more effective setting, play worship music in the background while your students work. Ask volunteers to share their responses.

As you wrap up the session, encourage students to conduct their own private worship services throughout the coming week, focusing their attention—even if it's just for a couple minutes at a time—on Jesus and giving him the praise and glory he deserves.

MORE MORE MORE

For Better or Worship

The topic of worship will be addressed in detail in session 5—and throughout the study, for that matter. If you'd prefer to use a different application for this session, focus on the portrayal of Jesus as a warrior in Revelation 19:11-21.

Use questions like these to get students thinking about the topic:

YOUTH WORKER SCRIPT

- Who or what is Jesus waging war against in Revelation 19?
- If Jesus is a warrior, what does that mean for those who follow him?
- What daily battles do we fight as Christians? What weapons do we have to help us?

Ask a volunteer to read Ephesians 6:10-18. Come up with a battle plan as a group, for dealing with temptation, doubt, fear, persecution, and other challenges we face every day. Talk about how truth, righteousness, readiness, peace, faith, the Word of God, and prayer can all be incorporated into the plan.

As you wrap up the meeting, ask students to keep journals in the week to come, recording the battles they encounter, their strategies for dealing with them, and the results—both good and bad—of their battles.

The Real You

For each of the following categories, write down some key words the person might use to describe you.

• *A casual acquaintance (perhaps a classmate, coworker, or youth group member who doesn't know you well)*

• *A close friend*

• *Your sibling (if you don't have a sibling, then your best friend in the world)*

• *Your parent (Mom or Dad—whichever one you're closest to)*

• *You*

The Real Messiah: What Did Jesus Do?

How much do you know about the Son of God? Here's a chance to test your knowledge. It's multiple choice, so you have at least a 25 percent chance to get each answer right!

1. What did Jesus instruct his followers to do when someone hit them?
   a. Give the person a chance to hit them again.
   b. Pray God would take vengeance on the person.
   c. Take the person to court and let a judge decide the matter.
   d. Hit the person back just as hard as they were hit—but no harder.

2. How did Jesus battle Satan when the Evil One tried to tempt him?
   a. He called for the earth to swallow Satan.
   b. He quoted God's Word.
   c. He condemned Satan to hell for eternity.
   d. He prayed for the archangel Michael to defend him.

3. When Jesus was on trial for his life, what did he do when the Jewish religious leaders brought in false witnesses to lie about him?
   a. He didn't even bother responding to the lies.
   b. He countered every lie with the truth of what he actually said and did.
   c. He warned that liars will eventually suffer the fires of hell.
   d. He told the witnesses he forgave them, but warned the Pharisees they would never be forgiven.

4. How did Jesus react to the gang of Roman soldiers who taunted and beat him and stole his clothes before his execution?
   a. He gave them three opportunities to stop their abuse before calling down fire from heaven to consume them.
   b. He struck them blind—at least temporarily.
   c. He reported them to their commanding officer, who had them thrown in prison.
   d. He allowed them to abuse him without lifting a finger to defend himself.

5. How did Jesus respond to the thief who challenged him to set himself and his fellow crucified prisoners free?
   a. He left it to another crucified prisoner to defend him.
   b. He freed the prisoners, but allowed himself to be executed.
   c. He spoke harshly to the man about his lack of faith.
   d. He requested his cross be moved away from the combative thief so he could spend his final hours on earth in prayer with his heavenly Father.

The Real Messiah: Jesus, Is That You?

Read each passage and answer the questions that follow.

Revelation 1:12-20

1. What are your impressions of the person John described?

2. There's a lot of symbolism in Revelation. What do the following descriptions symbolize?

    • *head and hair white as snow*

    • *eyes like blazing fire*

    • *feet like bronze glowing in a furnace*

    • *voice like the sound of rushing waters*

    • *a sharp, double-edged sword coming from his mouth*

3. What does it mean that the one described in the passage holds the seven churches in his hands (see verses 16 and 20)?

4. What was John's reaction to the person talking to him?

5. How would you react if you were to see the person John described standing right behind you?

6. What does it mean that the person is "the First and the Last" (verse 17)?

Revelation 5:1-14

7. *Sneak preview:* The opening of the seals on the scroll in verse 1 begins terrible judgments on the earth. (For more details check out Revelation 6.) Why was no one in heaven or on the earth worthy to open the scroll?

8. Why was John upset when no one came forward to open the scroll?

9. What are your impressions of the Lamb described in verse 6?

10. In the Bible the number seven represents perfection, completeness, or fullness. The horn is an ancient Jewish symbol for power or strength. With that in mind how would you explain the description of the Lamb in verse 6?

11. Why is the Lamb the only one worthy to open the seals on the scroll?

12. What is the reaction of the people, angels, and creatures in heaven to the Lamb?

Revelation 19:11-21

13. What are your impressions of the rider described in this passage?

14. Who would dare try to battle the armies of heaven?

15. Describe how you picture the battle between the armies of heaven and the armies of the earth.

16. What does the angel's birdcall in verses 17 and 18 tell us about the outcome of the battle?

17. Describe how you picture the after-battle judgment.

18. How would you use this passage to respond to Christians who get frustrated and discouraged by the evil they see around them?

The Big Question

What do the Son of Man in Revelation 1, the Lamb in Revelation 5, and the Rider on the White Horse in Revelation 19 all have in common?

3 If You Can't Say Something Nice...
Revelation 2

SOUND BITE

As far as Jesus is concerned, there's no such thing as a Fair Weather Christian—he expects complete commitment from his followers.

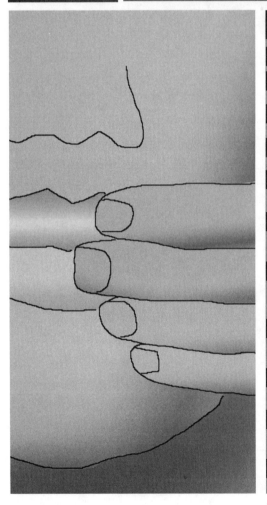

What You'll Need

- Bibles
- Pens
- Materials or props for stunts (optional)
- Stopwatch (optional)
- Slips of paper with dares written on them (optional)
- A container or hat to hold the dares (optional)
- A list of truths (relevant to this session) for students to divulge (optional)
- A short multiple-choice quiz (personalized to your youth room or surroundings) for each student
- Several silly or fun prizes to award the winners of the quiz
- Copies of **Through Thick and Thin** (pages 38-39) for each student
- Copies of **Jesus' Letter to Me** (page 40), one for each student

Where Do You Draw the Line?

This activity's a blatant rip-off of—uh, that is, *an affectionate homage to*—the reality TV show *Fear Factor*. If you're unfamiliar with the show, it's basically Truth or Dare without the truth option. Contestants are given challenges testing their courage and willingness to endure distasteful things. Those who successfully complete each challenge move on to the next one until only one person remains.

Common sense and your church's insurance policy will prohibit you from doing anything genuinely risky with your students. But with a little creativity, you can still come up with challenges testing their determination, if not their courage. You might want to ask the contestants to—

- Eat Twinkies whose fillings have been replaced with pickle relish.
- Sing "Twinkle, Twinkle, Little Star" and dance like ballerinas—wearing tights, tutus, and ballet slippers.
- Using only their teeth, pull 10 prunes from the bottom of a large bowl filled with ketchup and mustard—and then eat the prunes.
- Eat a whole can of anchovies each.
- Coat their hair with mayonnaise.

If you find the elimination process isn't going as quickly as you'd like, set a time limit for each challenge and eliminate students who don't complete it in time. You may want to use the following questions to help make the transition from the activity to the discussion:

YOUTH WORKER SCRIPT

- **What are some challenges you face on a daily basis? How do they compare to the challenges you faced in our game?**
- **Do you consider your Christian faith to be a challenge? Why or why not?**
- **We've seen how far you'd be willing to go in this game, but how far are you willing to go in your Christian life?**

Truth or Dare

Play a round—or a couple of rounds, depending on the size of your group—of Truth or Dare. Make sure each student has at least one opportunity to choose between answering a question with complete honesty (the truth) and performing a goofy stunt (the dare). Have students who choose dares draw pieces of paper from a container and then perform the stunts written on the paper. The dares should be mildly embarrassing, but nothing too personal or humiliating. For example you might dare students to—

- imitate a celebrity for thirty seconds
- drink baby formula from a bottle
- let someone in the group give them a hair and makeup makeover

Make sure at least some of the truth questions deal with the session topic in one form or another. For example you might ask students to—

- share three things they're committed to
- describe what a genuine commitment to Christ looks like
- talk about an obstacle that has negatively affected their personal commitment to Christ

You may want to use the following questions to help make the transition from the activity to the discussion:

YOUTH WORKER SCRIPT

- Are you ever challenged in life to tell the truth? Ever challenged in life to do something you don't really want to do?
- Do you consider your Christian faith to be a challenge? Why or why not?
- We've seen how far you'd be willing to go in this game, but how far are you willing to go in your Christian life?

To Commit or Not to Commit—That Is the Question

Prepare a short quiz for your students to take. The questions should involve information that is available to your students if they look around the youth room or church grounds. The quiz should also be multiple choice so if students don't feel like investigating the answers, they can take a guess.

Here are some examples of questions you might use:

YOUTH WORKER SCRIPT

- **How many electrical outlets are built into this room?**
- **How many parking spaces are painted onto the church parking lot?**
- **According to the instruction manual, what's the recommended motor oil weight for a 1993 Honda Civic?** (If you were to use this question, you would need to make sure you have a 1993 Honda Civic parked nearby, with its doors unlocked and an instruction manual in the glove compartment, for students who choose to investigate.)
- **What's the last song in our church hymnal?** (Obviously this question only works well if your church uses hymnals—otherwise you may want to use it as a trick question.)

Try to come up with five to 10 questions, depending on the time and resources available to you. Let students work in pairs or small groups to complete the quiz. When they're finished, reveal the answers. Then award prizes—not to the ones who got the most answers right, but to the ones who put the most effort into the activity.

You may want to use the following questions to discuss the activity:

YOUTH WORKER SCRIPT

- **On a scale of one to 10—1 is no effort at all and 10 is everything you had—how much effort did you put into the quiz? Why?** (If possible get explanations from those who followed every lead to its logical conclusion as well as those who never left their chairs. Chances are some students will admit to being motivated to follow leads because of the promise of reward or the simple thrill of competition.)

- **If this had been, say, a relay race, would you have put more or less effort into it?** (Prepare a list of different activities—everything from lifting weights to washing a car to choosing what to wear for a date—and let students call out "more" or "less" to indicate how much relative effort they would put into each activity.)

- **What situations bring out the best in you or inspire you to give the most effort? Why?**

- **Using the same scale we used earlier, how much effort would you say you put into living a life that's faithful and obedient to Christ?** (Encourage volunteers to respond, but don't force anyone to share.)

- **Why do respond in that way?** (Again encourage honest responses, but don't put anyone on the spot.)

MORE MORE MORE

To Commit or Not to Commit — That is the Question

Recruit a couple of Christian friends or church members to come in and briefly share their testimonies with the group. Have them focus especially on the rocky road they faced in developing genuine commitment in their walks with Christ— what they had to give up, how they did it, how they felt about it, how it affected their popularity, and how they feel about their decision now. Encourage them not to sugar-coat the truth or downplay the effects of genuine commitment to Christ.Jesus Christ.

Hitting the Book

Through Thick and Thin

Distribute pens and copies of **Through Thick and Thin** (pages 38-39) to your students while they're in the large group…then let 'em work in small groups to complete the sheet. Also, please gauge how much time you think this worksheet will take your group—feel free to highlight only key questions while eliminating others. When everyone's finished, ask volunteers to share their responses.

You may want to use the following comments to supplement your discussion of Revelation 2:

- Nowhere in the Bible does God promise an easy life to those who follow him. **In fact living the life to which Jesus calls his followers invites persecution.** (NOTE: Discuss what persecution is and means. A great source for you and your students are the *Jesus Freaks* books discussing those who've suffered for Christ throughout history.)

- **The fact that we face hardships as Christians isn't something to grumble about—it's something to celebrate.**

- **There's no shortage of people ready to tell us what's okay for us to do and tolerate and enjoy as Christians. We must be careful about who we listen to, though. False teachers are every bit as dangerous today as they were during Jesus' time.**

- **Though Jesus doesn't promise an endless vacation for those who follow him, he does promise to endlessly reward those who remain faithful to him.**

Making It Count

Jesus' Letter to Me

Distribute copies of **Jesus' Letter to Me** (page 40). Emphasize that there are no right or wrong answers for students to fill in. This is all about the details of their personal relationship with God. If you have volunteers who are comfortable sharing some of their responses, allow them to do so. Otherwise encourage students to display their letters in their lockers at school or on their bedroom mirror at home—any place where they will serve as reminders of the things they're doing right and the things they need to work on in their relationship with and commitment to Christ.

Through Thick and Thin

Read the passages from Revelation, and answer the questions that follow. Notice the four churches singled out in the Scripture.

Revelation 2:1-7

1. How does it make you feel to know that Jesus knows our deeds—the things we do and don't do every day? What should we do about those feelings?

2. What does it mean to tolerate a wicked person (verse 2)?

3. Why is it dangerous to our commitment to Christ to tolerate wicked people?

4. The Nicolaitans were people who called themselves Christians but believed they had the freedom to however they pleased. Why did Jesus hate their practices?

5. What are some things Christians must overcome (verse 7) in order to remain faithful to Christ?

6. How would you summarize Jesus' feelings about the church in Ephesus?

Revelation 2:8-11

7. Describe a time when you experienced persecution because of your Christian faith.

8. Be honest here: If you could be thrown in prison and executed for being a Christian, would it change the way you live your life? Why or why not?

9. If you were a member of the church of Smyrna, how would you feel about Jesus' encouragement? What about his rebuke?

10. What advice would you give to a Christian who's struggling to persevere during tough times?

Revelation 2:12-17

11. Jesus' phrase "where Satan has his throne" (verse 13) refers to the fact that Pergamum was the center of emperor worship in Asia. What evidence do you see in the world around you that Satan's reign is still going strong today?

12. Balaam was a false teacher who led the Israelites away from God. What are some examples of false teaching that lead Christians away from God today?

13. How would you summarize Jesus' feelings about the church in Pergamum?

Revelation 2:18-29

14. What does Jesus mean by the following words in verse 19:

  • *deeds*

  • *love*

  • *faith*

  • *service*

  • *perseverance*

15. What does Jesus' warning in verses 20 through 23 tell us about his feelings regarding false teachers?

16. What do Christians have to hold on to until Jesus comes back?

17. What's the reward for Christians who stay faithful to Jesus through thick and thin?

Jesus' Letter to Me

You've seen what Jesus had to say to the people in Ephesus, Smyrna, Pergamum, and Thyatira. What would he say to you? Fill in the blanks below to get a sense of how a letter from Jesus to you might read. If you're not comfortable writing personal information where someone might see it, use initials or code only you can understand.

To my servant [_____],

These are the words of the one who sees all. I know you have faced difficult situations recently, such as [_____]. I know the thoughts you've had about your situation. I know you've felt [_____]. I want you to know I've been by your side through it all—whether you realized it or not. Call on me and my strength the next time you [_____]. I will see you through.

I know your strengths, the way you can [_____], because I created you with them. I take joy in the fact that you have shown your faithfulness to me by [_____]. I want you to know you will be rewarded richly—and eternally—for your obedience.

I also know the struggles you face—the problem sins continuing to plague you. At the top of the list is [_____]. Remember I have called you to a life of holiness. Every time you fall back into sin, it affects every part of your life and your relationship with me, including [_____].

I have given you the power to remain faithful, obedient, and committed to me. In order to take advantage of that power, though, you must first [_____].

These are the words of the one who loves you and gave his life for you.

4 The Good, the Bad, and the Lukewarm *Revelation 3*

SOUND BITE

Anything less than extreme faithfulness and obedience is distasteful to God.

What You'll Need

- Bibles
- Pens
- A videotape or DVD of sports highlights (optional)
- TV or video-projection unit and VCR or DVD player (optional)
- Supplies for any competitive game (played in teams) familiar to your students (optional)
- A student or youth leader for each team, secretly assigned in advance as a mole or saboteur (optional)
- Several yummy prizes to award the winners of the game (optional)
- Flip chart or whiteboard and pens
- Copies of The Problem with Warm (page 47), one for each student
- Copies of Heat It Up (pages 48-49), one for each student

The Highlight Reel

As your students enter the meeting area, have a video of spectacular sports plays playing where everyone can see it. Most video stores carry several sports compilation tapes that should suit your need. If not just record your own. ESPN highlights the top plays of the day on its nightly *SportsCenter* program. (Be sure to screen the video for any objectionable material before you show it to your students.)

Discuss the tape and introduce the session topic, using questions like—

YOUTH WORKER SCRIPT

- **What motivates these athletes go to such extremes?**
- **Do you consider yourself an extreme person? If so, in what areas?**
- **What are some of the benefits of being an extreme person? What are some of the dangers?**

Kickoff Option 2

Dogging It

Play one of your students' favorite games—one guaranteed to get their competitive juices flowing. If you need to resort to bribery to get emotions running high, offer a desirable prize—like a bag of mini candy bars—to the winning team. As you divide the group into teams, make sure each team is assigned a mole—a player whose purpose is to subtly sabotage the team's chance of winning.

You'll need to recruit your moles before the meeting. Explain that all you want them to do is give a 50 percent effort—to play the game with about half of the intensity, competitiveness, and skill they would normally bring to it.

During the game pay attention to your students' reactions to the lackadaisical approach of the moles. Jot down specific words of encouragement, instruction, and frustration you hear. After the game reveal your arrangement with the moles to the group and thank the moles for their cooperation. You may want to use the following questions to guide your discussion of the activity:

- **How many of you gave one hundred percent in playing the game?** (Ask those who raise their hands to explain why they competed so hard.)
- **How did you feel about the people who seemed to be giving less than their best efforts during the game? Why?**
- **Name some other areas in which it's important to give a 100 percent effort.** (As students name specific areas, ask them to explain what they would consider to be 100 percent effort in each area.)

Focusing In

To the X-treme

Start your discussion by asking your students what images come to their minds when they hear the word *extreme*. Ask students to think of different contexts in which the word is used. If you need some prompts, you might ask students to describe—

- extreme mountain biking
- extreme skateboarding
- extreme surfing
- extreme climbing
- extreme skydiving

Wrap up the discussion by asking your students what they believe the term *Extreme Christianity* means. List your students' responses on a flip chart or whiteboard.

MORE MORE MORE

To the X-treme
Put your students' creativity to work. Let them work in pairs or small groups to introduce and demonstrate such new activities as extreme golf, extreme bowling, or even extreme solitaire. If you want to take this activity to the next level, give your students advance notice and ask them to videotape their demonstrations and then bring their tapes to the meeting. (Be sure to screen all tapes before showing them to the group.)

Hitting the Book

The Problem with Warm

Distribute pens and copies of **The Problem with Warm** (page 47) to your students while they're in the large group…then let 'em work in small groups to complete the sheet. Also, please gauge how much time you think this worksheet will take your group—feel free to highlight only key questions while eliminating others. When everyone's finished, ask volunteers to share their responses.

Let students work in small groups to complete the sheet. If you're short on time, you may also want to assign a section to each group or focus your discussion on the third section, the letter to Laodicea in Revelation 3:14-22.

You may want to use the following comments to supplement your discussion of Revelation 3:

YOUTH WORKER SCRIPT

- Our reputations are meaningless to Jesus if they don't match what's actually going on inside us. It's not hard to fool other people into believing we're something we're not, spiritually speaking. However, it's impossible to fool Jesus. He knows every thought we have, including our true motives for everything we do.

- Jesus encourages his followers to stay faithful, no matter how bleak things get. The more difficult our circumstances become, the closer we should draw to God.

- Jesus expects his followers to take their faithfulness, devotion, and obedience to him to the extreme. Lukewarm Christianity is disgusting to him. If our Christian faith isn't making a difference in our lives—as well as in the lives of the people around us—it's a dead faith.

- Extreme Christianity is being alive and on fire for God. It's being sold out to God 100 percent.

Heat It Up

Ask a volunteer to read Revelation 3:15-16 again. Then ask students what the difference is between being a *hot* Christian and a *lukewarm* Christian. The purpose of the question isn't necessarily to get verbal responses from your students, but to get students thinking about applying the principles of Revelation 3:15-16 to their lives.

Distribute copies of **Heat It Up** (pages 48-49). Let students work in pairs or small groups to complete the sheet. When everyone's finished, ask volunteers to share their answers. Write all of the *hot* responses on your flip chart or whiteboard.

As you wrap up the session, hand out index cards and ask students to write down two things they will do in the coming week to heat up their commitment to Christ. Encourage them to use the suggestions on the flip chart or whiteboard as inspiration. If you think your students would go for it, pair them up with accountability partners and encourage them to check on each other's progress during the week.

The Problem with Warm

Three Bible references. Fifteen questions. Hmm, what else does this sheet need? Some thoughtful responses from you would be nice—say, maybe, 15 of them!

Revelation 3:1-6

1. What did Jesus mean when he told the church in Sardis that though they had a reputation for being alive, they were actually dead?

2. Why is it important to have a good reputation among our fellow believers? Why is it potentially dangerous?

3. Describe the difference between being *alive* in Christ and being *dead* in Christ.

4. Based on Jesus' words in this passage, what advice would you give the church in Sardis? Be as specific as possible in your suggestions.

Revelation 3:7-13

5. How's it possible for someone of "little strength" (verse 8) to remain faithful to Christ?

6. Give an example of how a person might keep God's Word.

7. Give an example of how a person might deny Jesus' name.

8. What's your first reaction to Jesus' words in verse 11—"I am coming soon"?

9. Describe what Jesus liked about the church in Philadelphia.

10. List the promises Jesus made to the church in Philadelphia.

Revelation 3:14-22

11. What was the problem with the church in Laodicea?

12. What does it mean to be a lukewarm follower of Christ?

13. What's the problem with being lukewarm?

14. What's Jesus' reaction to lukewarm Christians?

15. How does a person become hot in his relationship with Christ?

Heat It Up

Explain how a lukewarm Christian and a hot Christian might respond to each of the following situations. Be as specific as possible, especially with your hot responses.

1. Your youth group leader challenges you to begin a personal Bible study.

    Lukewarm Christian response—

    Hot Christian response—

2. Your neighbor asks you why you go to church every Sunday.

    Lukewarm Christian response—

    Hot Christian response—

3. The girl behind you in English class mentions her grandmother just died.

    Lukewarm Christian response—

    Hot Christian response—

4. Your pastor announces the local homeless shelter needs donations and workers.

    Lukewarm Christian response—

    Hot Christian response—

5. Your best friend invites you to a party you know is gonna get out of control.

Lukewarm Christian response—

Hot Christian response—

6. The person you're dating tells you it's time to take your relationship to the next level, sexually speaking.

Lukewarm Christian response—

Hot Christian response—

7. You find out a former friend of yours is now spreading some nasty rumors about you at school.

Lukewarm Christian response—

Hot Christian response—

8. Everything in your life seems to be going wrong.

Lukewarm Christian response—

Hot Christian response—

Before the Throne
Revelation 4-5

SOUND BITE

Genuine worship isn't something we grudgingly offer God for an hour or so a week—it's the natural, passionate response to recognizing and acknowledging who God truly is.

What You'll Need

- Bibles
- Pens
- Several adults or volunteer staffers to act as cheer competition judges (optional)
- Blank scorecards and large markers for judges (optional)
- A mouth-watering, edible prize to award the winners of the cheer competition (optional)
- Music CDs from a wide variety of genres (optional)
- CD player
- Lots of index cards
- Flip chart or whiteboard and pens
- Copies of **Say It Loud and Say It Proud** (page 55), one for each student
- Copies of **Worship 101** (pages 56-57), one for each student
- Worship music CD

Kickoff Option 1

Gimme a G!

Divide the group into squads of three or four for a cheerleading competition. Announce the squads will be given a few minutes to brainstorm their own cheers—and routines to go with them. If you have any actual cheerleaders in the group, ask them to demonstrate a simple cheer and routine to help inspire the other squads.

To increase the level of difficulty another notch, announce the squads must come up with a cheer and routine based on the topic of your choice. Depending on how mischievous you're feeling, you may choose anything from croquet to yard work as your topic. Just make sure you give your teams something they can get creative with. If you want to go all out for the activity, invite a "celebrity panel" (or anyone you can round up at the last minute) to judge the competition—perhaps by holding up scorecards after each routine.

If you think some of your students might be reluctant to participate, offer an irresistible, mouth-watering prize—such as cheesecake or chocolate chip cookies to the squad presenting the best routine.

Afterward discuss the competition and introduce the session topic of worship, using questions like—

YOUTH WORKER SCRIPT

- What if I had given you "God" as a topic for your cheers? Would it have been easier or harder to come up with a cheer for him than it was for the topic I gave you? Explain.
- Name some things you might mention in a cheer about God.
- How do you usually express your feelings about God to him?

Kickoff Option 2

Groovin'

Before the meeting you'll need to round up a stack of CDs from several different musical genres—rock, hip-hop, pop, metal, country, bluegrass, folk, jazz, opera, big band, classical, polka, and anything else you can find. To start the session play 30 seconds or so of a cut from each CD. (Be sure you screen all cuts for objectionable lyrics before playing them for the group.)

Don't explain what you're doing; just pay attention to students' reactions to the music. Watch especially for physical reactions—students nodding their heads, bouncing in their seats, tapping their feet, playing air guitar, and so forth.

Afterward ask those who were the most exuberant in their music appreciation to explain why they reacted as they did, and chances are someone will suggest it's just a natural reaction. Talk briefly about other natural reactions people experience. If no one else mentions it, point out people laugh at funny commercials, scream or jump during horror movies, and cry at the end of tearjerker novels.

Continue with questions like—

YOUTH WORKER SCRIPT

- **Does worship come naturally to people? Why or why not?**
- **Is worship is something that should come naturally to people? Why or why not?**

Focusing In

That's What I Like about You

Distribute pencils and index cards. Each student will need one index card. (If your group is gargantuan, you may want to divide into small groups for this activity—and try to put friends in the same groups, otherwise they may no know others well enough to discuss thoughtfully and sincerely.) Instruct students to write on each card the name of a student and a positive quality or characteristic about that person. Encourage students to put some thought into their answers and to be sincere in their affirmation. They'll need to fill out one card for every person in the group or small group.

Collect the cards and separate them into piles, one for each student. Read the affirming statements one at a time in each pile and let students guess who you're describing. If your students cooperate, this activity can go a long way toward building confidence in the lives of those who need it most.

After you've gone through all the cards, ask your students to name positive qualities and characteristics about God. Don't settle for generic answers, though. For example if someone says, "God is good," ask him to identify something specific God has done or promised that makes him good. Write your students' responses on a flip chart or whiteboard so you can refer to them later.

WORTHY OF WORSHIP

That's What I Like About You

You can turn the attribute-naming exercise into a game with a pair of dice imprinted with letters (like the Boggle game) and a stopwatch. Let students take turns rolling the dice and naming attributes of God—or things to praise him for—beginning with those two letters. Correct answers equal 1,000 points.

Hitting the Book

Say It Loud and Say It Proud

Distribute pens and copies of **Say It Loud and Say It Proud** (page 55) to your students while they're in the large group…then let 'em work in small groups to complete the sheet. Also, please gauge how much time you think this worksheet will take your group—feel free to highlight only key questions while eliminating others. You may want to use the following comments to supplement your discussion of Revelation 4-5:

YOUTH WORKER SCRIPT

- The extreme examples of worship described in Revelation 4-5 may be explained by the fact that the worshiping creatures have front row seats to God's glory. The result of such proximity to God himself seems to be an irresistible compulsion to praise him. In other words the closer someone gets to God, the more natural—and perhaps even compelling—worship becomes.

- Our closeness to God—or lack thereof—is reflected in our worship. The more intimate our relationship is with him, the more aspects of his nature we will see; the more aspects of his nature we see, the more eager we'll be to offer him praise and glory in response.

- Worship is the eternal destiny of every Christian—you could call it the national pastime of heaven. If that seems like a less-than-exciting prospect, it's because we don't understand what true worship is.

Making It Count

Worship 101

Distribute copies of **Worship 101** (pages 56-57). Let students work in pairs or small groups to complete the sheet. Discuss the worksheet as a large group. Then wrap up your session with a mini worship service. Play familiar praise choruses or Christian songs to set the mood. Encourage students to sing along with the worshipful spirit described in Revelation 4-5. Ask volunteers to share specific praises and Bible passages from their repro sheet. Close the service in prayer, asking God to bless your students' desire and commitment to praise and honor him and to help them understand the difference genuine worship can make in their lives.

WORTHY OF WORSHIP

Worship 101

For an unforgettable worship experience, let your students plan and execute the mini-service themselves. Assign different elements of the service—prayer, Bible reading, personal praise, testimonies, and music—to different individuals or pairs within the group. Those individuals or pairs will then be responsible for either fulfilling those roles themselves or finding someone else to do it. Make sure each student has a vital role in your worship planning and execution.

FOR MORE INFO...

Check out the ton of worship service ideas in two fab resources, *The Book of Uncommon Prayer* and *Worship Services for Youth Groups* (www.YouthSpecialties.com).

Say It Loud and Say It Proud

Can you guess what you're supposed to do on this sheet? Hint: It has something to do with looking up Bible verses and responding to questions.

Revelation 4:1-11

1. What do the precious stones—jasper, carnelian, and emerald—and rainbows suggest about God's throne (verse 3)?

2. What do the flashes of lightning and peals of thunder suggest (verse 5)?

3. Describe how you picture God's throne, based on what you understand from verses 2 to 11.

4. What does the description of God's throne tell us about God?

5. Why do you suppose the creatures described in verses 6 through 9 never stop praising God?

6. What, specifically, are the creatures praising and honoring God for?

7. According to the 24 elders, why is God "worthy...to receive glory and honor and power" (verse 11)?

8. What's your opinion of the heavenly style of worship described in Revelation 4?

Revelation 5:1-14

9. Who is the Lamb—the Lion of the tribe of Judah, the Root of David?

10. According to the 24 elders, why was the Lamb worthy to receive praise and honor (verse 9)?

11. How would you reword the song in verses 9 and 10 to express your own feelings about the Lamb's sacrifice?

12. Describe how you picture the gathering of worshiping creatures in verses 11 through 14.

13. What does this passage reveal about worship in heaven?

14. Why are the creatures of heaven so enthusiastic in their worship of God?

15. What lessons can earthly worshipers learn from their heavenly counterparts?

Worship 101

Worship can take place anywhere and at any time. Meaningful worship, however, requires some preparation on our part. Think of this sheet as a "worship preparation" checklist.

1. Take care of any personal problems with other people that might interfere with your worshiping spirit.

"Therefore, if you are offering your gift at the altar and there remember that your brother has something against you, leave your gift there in front of the altar. First go and be reconciled to your brother; then come and offer your gift" (Matthew 5:23-24).

Things I need to make right with other people before I can have genuine fellowship with God—

2. Ask forgiveness for sins that will interrupt your fellowship with God.

"If we confess our sins, he is faithful and just and will forgive us our sins and purify us from all unrighteousness" (1 John 1:9).

Things I need to confess in order to make my relationship with God right again—

3. Identify specific things to praise God for.

"Because of the Lord's great love we are not consumed, for his compassions never fail. They are new every morning; great is your faithfulness" (Lamentations 3:22-23).

Things I need to praise and worship God for—

4. Spend some time in Scripture.

"Your word is a lamp to my feet and a light for my path" (Psalm 119:105).

A Bible verse or promise especially meaningful to me right now—

5. Worship can take many forms!

"David, wearing a linen ephod, danced before the LORD with all his might" (2 Samuel 6:14)

"David and all the Israelites were celebrating with all their might before God, with songs and with harps, lyres, tambourines, cymbals and trumpets." (1 Chronicles 13:8)

A Bible verse or promise especially meaningful to me right now—

6

Time's Up
Revelation 6; 8-9;16

SOUND BITE

God has been patient with the human race for centuries, giving everyone a chance to come to him—but he won't allow evil to go unpunished forever.

What You'll Need

- • Bibles
- • Pens
- • Equipment or props for several wacky stunts (optional)
- • Copies of a crossword puzzle or word search for each student (optional)
- • Stopwatch
- • Several silly or fun prizes to award winners
- • Several artistically inclined students or volunteer staff to illustrate specific verses on posters
- • Copies of **You Be the Judge** (page 65), one for each student
- • Copies of **Judgment Days** (pages 66-69), one for each student
- • Copies of **Judgment Days Defined** (pages 70-71), one for each student (optional)
- • Preparation for discussing your church's eschatological viewpoints with students as you review **Judgment Days Defined** (optional)
- • Radio with manual tuner
- • Index cards for each student

Kickoff Option

Beat the Clock

For this activity you'll need to come up with a variety of timed stunts for your students to complete individually or in teams. Here are some ideas to get you started:

- Sort a bowl full of marbles by color while wearing ultra-dark sunglasses.
- Assemble a 24-piece jigsaw puzzle using thumbs only.
- Complete 12 somersaults without touching anyone or anything in the room—except the floor, of course.
- Open a book—while wearing boxing gloves—to page 100 and read the first two sentences.
- Tag everyone in the room. (Encourage the rest of your students to avoid being tagged at all costs.)
- Make 10 free throws using paper wads and a trash can at least 10 feet away.

As much as possible, test each stunt yourself before the meeting so you can assign it an appropriate—yet challenging—time limit. In other words you want your students to feel the pressure while they're competing. Award prizes to those who successfully complete their assignments within the given time limit.

Use the idea of time running out during your stunts to segue into the session topic. Point out there's a time limit for sin, and one day God will pronounce his final judgment on all evildoers.

Kickoff Option

A Puzzling Development

If you don't have the time or equipment for the *Beat the Clock* activity, try a simple puzzle-solving contest. Distribute copies of a crossword puzzle or word search, and let students work in pairs to try to complete the puzzle within a specified time limit. Award prizes to those who are successful, but do everything you can to create tension during the activity so students have a sense of time running out on them.

Afterward ask volunteers to share experiences in which they actually felt the pressure of time and talk about how they performed under that pressure. Introduce the session topic by pointing out there's a time limit for sin in the world, and one day God will pronounce his final judgment on all evildoers.

Beat the Clock or A Puzzling Development

To introduce the theme of apocalypse, you could also play some key scenes of disaster and destruction from movies such as *Armageddon, Deep Impact, Dante's Peak, Earthquake, Meteor, When Time Ran Out,* or anything else you can find at your local video store. Use the clips as reference points in your discussion of the judgments described in Revelation 6, 8-9, and 16.

Focusing In

You Be the Judge

Before the meeting recruit a couple of artistically gifted students to create posters for you. One poster should be based on this phrase in Romans 6:23—"the wages of sin is death"; the other should be based on the words of Romans 12:19 (NKJV)—"'Vengeance is mine, I will repay,' says the Lord." Ask your artists to include the text on their posters, and then display the posters prominently in the room.

Distribute pencils and copies of **You Be the Judge** (page 65). Let students work in pairs or small groups to complete the sheet. When everyone's finished, ask volunteers to share their responses. If you find students have markedly different responses to a certain situation, encourage a little debate over how serious the offense really is.

You may want to use the following questions to guide your discussion of the sheet:

YOUTH WORKER SCRIPT

- Are the people in these situations equally guilty? Were they deserving of equal punishment?
- What did you base your judgments on? What situations were the most offensive to you? Why?
- Explain the concept of letting the punishment fit the crime.
- How would God judge these scenarios? Explain your answer.

Hitting the Book

Judgment Days

Distribute pens and copies of **Judgment Days** (pages 66-69) to your students while they're in the large group…then let 'em work in small groups to complete the sheet. Also, please gauge how much time you think this worksheet will take your group—feel free to highlight only key questions while eliminating others.

Divide the group into four study teams, and assign each team one section of the sheet to complete. Then ask a volunteer from each team to summarize the team's passage and responses for the rest of the group.

You may want to use the following comments to supplement your discussion of Revelation 6, 8–9, and 16:

YOUTH WORKER SCRIPT

- Anyone who believes God is soft on—even indifferent to—sin and evil should take a hard look at the judgments in these passages. The fact that he gives people a chance to come to him shouldn't be taken advantage of. When his judgment comes—and it will come—the results will be horrific. Some people will discover too late just how seriously God takes sin.

- Many Christians believe the seal judgments, trumpet judgments, and especially the bowl judgments will occur in fairly rapid succession. In other words people won't have time to recover from one judgment before the next one hits. The results will be unimaginable destruction and devastation.

- The judgments aren't random acts of violence on God's part. He has a specific purpose and intent for every judgment. In many cases—including the water turning to blood, painful sores, locusts, and darkness—the judgments in Revelation are reminiscent of the plagues he afflicted on Egypt in Exodus 7-12.

- With these judgments God demonstrates not only his holiness and justice but also his unlimited power and his control over the natural world. Who else could hurl a mountain into the sea like a pebble?

LET'S GET THEOLOGICAL

Judgment Days

At some point during your discussion of Revelation 6, 8-9, and 16, you may want to distribute copies of **Judgment Days Defined** (pages 70-71) to each student. The amount of time you spend talking about the terms on the sheet will depend on how much eschatology you want to expose your students to, time available, and students' questions.

You might want to explain that many Christians believe the judgments of God described in Revelation 6; 8-9; and 16 will occur during a seven-year period known as the Tribulation. Point out some Christians—known as *pretribulationists*—believe Christians will experience the Rapture (being instantaneously transported to heaven) before the judgments take place. Some Christians—known as *midtribulationists*—believe the Rapture will occur at the midpoint of the Tribulation, three-and-a-half years into it, just before things get really scary. Other Christians—known as *posttribulationists*—believe Jesus won't return until after the Tribulation, meaning Christians who are living at that time will experience all of the judgments of those passages.

At the very least you should be prepared to share your church's teachings regarding the interpretation and timeline of Revelation and answer any questions your students may have.

Making It Count

Interference

As you wrap up the session, say something like—

YOUTH WORKER SCRIPT

As Christians we don't have to worry about eternal judgment for our sins. Jesus gave his life to pay the punishment for sin once and for all. When we accept that truth and make Jesus Savior and Lord of our lives, we're made righteous by God and our sins are forgiven—forever.

That doesn't mean, however, that sin has no effect on our lives. It does. Sin usually has consequences even after God forgives us, and it interferes with our relationship with God.

To illustrate the idea of interference, turn on a radio and listen to some music for a few moments. Then slowly change the frequency—by turning the tuner knob or pressing the tuner button—so the clear reception is gradually replaced by broken reception and, finally, complete static.

Continue with—

YOUTH WORKER SCRIPT

That's what happens when we let sin creep in to our lives. Our relationship with God becomes full of static—like you hear on a car radio that's moving away from its station's signal. The more we give in to temptation, the more distant we get from his Word and the less clear his will becomes for our lives.

The Bible promises us nothing can permanently separate believers from God's love. But if there's one thing these chapters in Revelation prove, it's that God takes sin seriously. And if we care about our relationship with him, we should take sin seriously too.

Distribute index cards and ask students to write down a specific sin that may be interfering with their relationship with God. If students are embarrassed or reluctant to write things others might see, suggest they use code instead. Set aside a few minutes for students to pray about their sins, asking God not only to forgive them, but also to clear out any static in their relationship with him.

Before you close the session, remind students that praying for forgiveness is only the first step in dealing with sin; there's also the matter of repentance—turning away from the attitudes, temptations, and situations that led to the sin in the first place. And stress that their own willpower isn't enough—we all need to rely on the Holy Spirit for help, nourishment from Scripture, and support and accountability from other Christians!

Encourage students to write on the back of their index cards two or three specific steps they will take this week to prevent themselves from falling back into the same sin again.

Give volunteers a chance to share their ideas with the group, but don't put anyone on the spot. As students leave remind them to post their ideas in a place where they will see them often.

WORTHY OF WORSHIP

Interference

If you have some extra time at the end of your meeting, lead your students in an impromptu worship session focusing on God's power. Encourage students to praise God for the fact that the entire physical universe is under his control. If it's his will for a star to crash to earth or for the sun to lose a third of its brightness or for water to turn to blood, no laws of physics—or anything else for that matter—can prevent it from happening.

You Be the Judge

Read each of the following scenarios and then determine an appropriate sentence for each one. We're not necessarily talking about prison sentences here or punishment in the legal sense of the word—we're looking for your idea of justice in each situation. So be as creative as you want in assigning punishments.

1. A 10-year-old boy shoplifts a game cartridge.

2. A 16-year-old girl steals her best friend's boyfriend.

3. A 17-year-old student leader in the youth group smokes a joint at a party.

4. A 46-year-old homeless man smashes a store window and steals a coat for the winter.

5. A 20-year-old college junior cheats on a midterm exam.

6. A 28-year-old drunk driver loses control of her car and seriously injures a tow truck driver.

7. A 28-year-old drunk driver lies about whether he's had anything to drink when he's stopped by a police officer—and doesn't even get a ticket.

8. A 13-year-old boy punches the classmate who's been bullying him all year.

9. A 15-year-old girl passes along an embarrassing rumor she heard about one of her volleyball teammates.

10. A 35-year-old man with a wife and two young children has an affair with one of his coworkers.

From *Creative Bible Lessons in Revelation.* Copyright © 2003 Youth Specialties. Permission to reproduce this page granted only for use in buyer's own youth group. This page can be downloaded for free from the Web site for this book: www.YouthSpecialties.com/store/downloads (password: **rev**).

Time's Up   65

Judgment Days

You could try answering the following questions without reading the passages first, but your responses probably wouldn't make much sense. That's why we recommend reading the passages first.

Revelation 6:1-17

1. What happens when the first seal is broken?

2. When you think of a conqueror, what images come to mind?

3. What happens when the second seal is broken?

4. What would be the result of removing peace from the earth (verse 4)?

5. What happens when the third seal is broken?

6. The creatures' announcement in verse 6 suggests the price of food will increase 10 times. What would the results be today if people were forced to pay 10 times the normal price for food?

7. What happens when the fourth seal is broken?

8. Describe what it would be like if one out of every four people in your school suddenly died.

9. What happens when the fifth seal is broken?

10. Have you ever asked a question similar to the one the martyrs ask in verse 10? If so, what were the circumstances that made you ask it?

11. What happens when the sixth seal is broken?

12. Why do you suppose the people described in verses 15 through 17 respond as they do to the events happening around them?

Revelation 8:1-13

13. What happens when the seventh seal is broken?

14. Why do you suppose the inhabitants of heaven grow quiet for half an hour?

15. What happens when the first trumpet is sounded (verse 7)?

16. Describe some of the consequences of losing one third of the earth's plant life.

17. What happens when the second trumpet is sounded?

18. How do you picture this judgment occurring?

19. What happens when the third trumpet is sounded?

20. What would be some of the results of having one third of the earth's drinking water polluted?

21. What happens when the fourth trumpet is sounded?

22. How would people respond to seeing heavenly bodies being wiped out of the sky?

Revelation 9:1-21

23. What happens when the fifth trumpet is sounded?

24. Describe how you picture life on earth during the time of the fifth trumpet judgment.

25. What does it mean that "men will seek death, but will not find it; they will long to die, but death will elude them" in verse 6?

26. What happens when the sixth trumpet is sounded?

26. How do you picture the angels of death?

27. Why do you suppose the survivors of the various plagues and judgments continue in their wicked ways, even after everything they've witnessed and experienced?

Revelation 16:1-21

28. What happens when the first bowl is poured out?

29. Describe what it would be like to be covered with painful sores.

30. What happens when the second bowl is poured out?

31. What would be the effects of all marine life dying?

32. What happens when the third bowl is poured out?

33. Why is the judgment of bloody drinking water appropriate?

34. What happens when the fourth bowl is poured out?

35. Why do you suppose people choose to curse God for his judgments instead of repenting (verse 9)?

36. What happens when the fifth bowl is poured out?

37. How would people respond to the world being thrown into total darkness?

38. What happens when the sixth bowl is poured out?

39. How are the demons able to convince the kings of the world to do battle with God (14)?

40. What happens when the seventh bowl is poured out?

41. Describe how you picture the earth after the seventh bowl judgment is finished.

Judgment Days Defined

No matter how little you know about the book of Revelation or end-times events, chances are you've heard terms such as antichrist, rapture, and tribulation. But what do they mean? And what do they have to do with the things we're talking about in this study? To help answer that question, here's a simple glossary of terms and concepts that will clue you into a better understanding of what the book of Revelation says and how different Christians interpret it.

666
This number refers to the brand of the Beast, a mark on a person's hand or forehead indicating loyalty to the Antichrist. Only those people who are branded with the number will be allowed to buy and sell goods—including food (Revelation 13:16-18; 19:20).

Antichrist
This figure of wickedness establishes himself as Jesus' enemy and brings about the Tribulation before he's defeated at Armageddon. He's also referred to in Scripture as the *little horn* (Daniel 7:8-27), the *man of lawlessness* (2 Thessalonians 2:2-4), and the *Beast* (Revelation 13:1-10; 19:19-20).

Armageddon
This is where the Antichrist and the kings of the earth gather for one last great battle against God (Revelation 16:16). Jesus returns to earth with the armies of heaven to defeat the forces of evil (Revelation 19:11-21).

Dragon
This is another name for Satan. He's also called a *huge red fiery serpent*. The fact that he's described as having seven heads and crowns, 10 horns, and a large tail that sweeps away stars (Revelation 12:3-6) suggests he's extremely powerful. Ultimately, though, he will be thrown into the lake of fire forever (Revelation 20:2, 10).

Eschatology
This is the branch of theology focusing on end-times events and prophecies.

False Prophet
Also known as the *second beast* or the *beast out of the earth*, he's responsible for persuading the world to worship the Beast (Revelation 13:11-18). He establishes the mark of the Beast—*666*—and it allows only those who are branded to buy and sell goods. He's capable of performing miracles to support his claims (Revelation 13:11-15). Eventually he's thrown into the lake of fire (Revelation 19:19-21; 20:10).

Great White Throne Judgment
At this terrible event of reckoning, unsaved people from throughout the ages are evaluated according to the things they did on earth in order to determine their punishment in hell. And believers in Jesus are recorded in the Book of Life and given eternal life (Revelation 20:11-15).

Lake of Burning Sulfur
Also known as the *lake of fire*, this is the final destination for unsaved people, one that will last forever (Revelation 20:10).

Lamb of God
This symbolic name for Jesus refers to the fact that he was slaughtered as a sacrifice for sin (Revelation 5:5-14; 17:14; 21:22-23).

Millennium
This refers to the 1,000-year reign of Christ (Revelation 20:1-7) during which Satan is bound. Some Christians—known as *premillennialists*—believe Jesus will return to earth to establish his visible kingdom and will physically reign as king for 1,000 years. Some Christians—known as *postmillennialists*—believe the millennium refers to the time it takes the church to progressively spread the news of Jesus throughout the world. They believe Christ will return after the millennial period is over. Other Christians—known as *amillennialists*—believe the 1,000-year earthly reign of Christ won't be a literal one on earth. They believe the events described in Revelation 20 are occurring now in the church, through Jesus' victory over Satan.

New Jerusalem
Also known as the *Holy City* (Revelation 21:1-3), the New Jerusalem will be part of the new earth God creates for eternity. The city—which is described as being cube-shaped—will descend from heaven. The Lamb's throne, the Tree of Life, and the River of Life are all contained in the city.

Rapture
This is the event at which living and dead believers will be taken in the clouds to meet Jesus in the air when he returns (1 Thessalonians 4:17). Believers will receive their new resurrection bodies at the Rapture (1 Corinthians. 15:51-55; Philippians 3:21). Some Christians—known as *pretribulationists*—believe the Rapture will occur before the Tribulation, and Christians will be spared the terror on earth. Some Christians—known as *midtribulationists*—believe the Rapture will occur at the midpoint of the Tribulation, three-and-a-half years into it. Other Christians—known as *posttribulationists*—believe Jesus won't return until after the Tribulation, and Christians who are living at that time will experience all of the judgments described in Revelation 6; 8-9; and 16.

Second Coming
The Second Coming refers to Christ's promised return (John 14:3; Titus 2:13). Some people believe the Rapture and the Second Coming are two different events, that Christ will come back to meet his Church in the air at the Rapture and then wait seven years before making his Second Coming to establish his kingdom on earth. Other people believe the terms *Rapture* and *Second Coming* refer to the same event.

Tribulation
This term refers to a future period of unprecedented evil and judgment (Daniel 12:1). During the Tribulation the Antichrist will wage war against God's people (Revelation 13:1-18). In turn God will rain punishment after punishment on the earth and its inhabitants. Scripture suggests the Tribulation lasts seven years, divided into two 3½ year periods.

7

Revelation 6, 8-9,16

God is infinitely more complex than we can possibly imagine—basing our opinion of him on one or two of his attributes will prevent us from recognizing and fully appreciating what he's really like.

What You'll Need

- Bibles
- Pens
- TV or video-projection unit and VCR or DVD player with remote control (optional)
- A videotape or DVD movie your students are unfamiliar with (optional)
- Several moles secretly assigned in advance to sabotage your game of Telephone (optional)
- A special item hidden in a box your students would not readily identify
- A dozen index cards bearing mysterious clues about your special item
- A silly or fun prize to award the student who identifies the special item first
- Copies of **The Big Picture: Limited Perspectives** (page 78), one for each student
- Copies of **The Big Picture: Match Game** (page 79), one for each student

Pardon the Interruption

Begin the meeting with a "random-scene" movie screening. If possible choose a movie you're familiar with, but your students have never seen or heard of. (You'll also need to make sure you choose a movie without any objectionable scenes in it.)

Start off by showing a 15-second clip of the first scene of the movie. Then forward the tape or DVD to a random scene approximately 20 minutes in to the movie. Play another 15-second clip, then forward it to a random scene approximately 40 minutes in to the movie. Continue this pattern of viewing 15 seconds of every 20 minutes of the movie until you reach the credits.

Afterward ask students to try to make sense of what they saw by filling in the blanks between scenes. Encourage them to reconstruct as much of the movie's plot as possible, based on the scenes they saw. You might also ask them to weigh in on what particular characters were like. After several students have offered their opinions, reveal what actually happened in the movie, as well as what the major characters were like.

Segue into the session topic by pointing out that just as your students didn't have enough information to draw an accurate conclusion of what the movie was like, many people don't have enough information to draw an accurate conclusion of what God's like.

Telephone Sabotage

This is the classic game of Telephone, in which players sit in a circle and pass a message from person to person—with a twist. For this game you'll need to recruit one or two moles to sabotage the process.

Here's how the game works. You will sit in the circle with your students and whisper a message to the person sitting on your right. That person will then whisper the message to the next person, who will pass it on to the next person—repeating the message in that way, all the way around the circle. Each player may relay the message only once; no repeating allowed. When the person on your left whispers the message to you, compare the finished version with the original one to see how it mutated. The results are often pretty funny.

If you want to get your students' competitive juices flowing, announce you will award fabulous prizes if the group manages to transport a message word for word around the circle. Your moles, however, should make sure no message makes it around the circle intact. Encourage them to mumble, talk as fast as they can, or alter words slightly when passing along the message—anything to ensure maximum confusion and minimum understanding.

After a few rounds, identify the moles to the group and reveal their assignment. Afterward point out that what's true of the Telephone game is true of our notions about God: *Our understanding is only as reliable and trustworthy as the means by which we come to it.* That's why all of our opinions concerning what God's like should come straight from his Word.

Focusing In

Get a Clue

Bring in a box with a mystery item inside. Announce that if your students were to correctly guess the mystery item within a certain time limit (perhaps 10 minutes), they would win a prize. Then explain that since you're such a wonderful human being, you've hidden clue cards throughout your meeting area to help your students identify the mystery item. The more clues they find in the allotted time, the better their chances will be of correctly guessing what the item is.

Before the meeting you'll need to prepare and hide several clue cards giving a vague hint as to what the mystery item is. For example if your mystery item were a tennis ball, you might write each of the following clues—minus the parenthetical statements of course—on index cards:

- fuzzy
- branded (*a reference to its logo*)
- colored
- returnable
- sporty
- canned
- high-speed
- judged (*a reference to line judges determining whether a ball is in or out*)
- in
- out

Make sure the cards are well hidden. Ideally your students should be able to find no more than half of them in the time allotted. Also make sure the clues aren't too obvious. You don't want students to be able to identify the mystery item based on one or two clues. In order to prevent students from simply firing a rapid succession of wild guesses at you, limit them to two or three official guesses as a group.

Afterward you might want to segue into the session topic with the following questions:

YOUTH WORKER SCRIPT

- If your students were successful in guessing the mystery item, ask—**How many clues did you need to put together in order to figure out the big picture?**
- If your students were unsuccessful, ask—**What prevented you from seeing the big picture of what was inside the box? Which clues threw you off?**
- **What clues do we have to figure out the big picture of who God is and what he's like?**

MORE MORE MORE

Get a Clue

If you don't have the time or mental energy to prepare clue cards, introduce the topic with a jigsaw puzzle instead. Put together the outer frame of a 48-piece jigsaw puzzle and then hide the interior pieces. Give students a certain amount of time to find the pieces and identify the picture in the puzzle. Obviously the more pieces they find, the better chance they'll have of identifying the picture. To introduce the session topic, point out the more *pieces* of information we have about God's nature, the better we'll be able to see the big picture of what he's like.

Hitting the Book

The Big Picture

Distribute pens and copies of **The Big Picture: Limited Perspectives** (page 78) to your students while they're in the large group…then let 'em work in small groups to complete the sheet. Also, please gauge how much time you think this worksheet will take your group—feel free to highlight only key questions while eliminating others. When they're finished, ask volunteers to share their responses. You may want to use the following questions to guide your discussion of the sheet:

- **What are some other misconceptions people have about God?**
- **Where do those misconceptions come from?**
- **What effects can misconceptions about God have on our lives?**

If no one else mentions it, point out that some people picture God as a kindly grandfather in the sky. Others think of him as the absentee landlord of the universe, the one who got things started at creation and then took off, leaving us to fend for ourselves. Still others picture God as some ultra-malleable being who's whatever we want him to be. Each of these misconceptions is equally inaccurate and equally damaging to a healthy relationship with God.

You may want to suggest—if no one else does—that most misconceptions about God result from a lack of accurate information about him or the tendency to bring him down to our level and think of him in human terms.

Point out that our beliefs concerning God's nature affect not only the way we interpret Scripture and communicate with him, but also the way we portray him to others. If we emphasize his justice and holiness at the expense of his love, we may discourage people from wanting to get to know him. If we emphasize his love at the expense of his justice and holiness, we may cause people to underestimate the seriousness of sin.

Distribute pencils and copies of **The Big Picture: Match Game** (page 79), and let students work in pairs or small groups to identify God's attributes. When they're finished reveal the answers: *1-b; 2-e; 3-a; 4-j; 5-i; 6-d; 7-h; 8-f; 9-g; 10-c.* Briefly discuss what each attribute reveals about God—and what it means to us, personally speaking.

You may want to use the following comments to supplement your discussion:

YOUTH WORKER SCRIPT

- **God's attributes exist in perfect harmony. He doesn't love on some days and not on others. He's always perfectly loving, perfectly just, perfectly holy, and so forth. His attributes never interfere with or cancel out each other.**
- **The fact that we can't fully understand the perfection of God's attributes shouldn't keep us from acknowledging and praising him for them. Keep in mind we're using finite brains to understand infinite concepts.**

- Our understanding of God's attributes should be reflected in our lives and in our interaction with him. For example if we truly believe God is holy, we should take all necessary steps to remove sin from our lives. If we believe he's loving, we should feel comfortable going to him with all of our problems. If we believe he's all-knowing, we should hand over the reins of our life to him and let him lead us.

making It Count

Getting to Know You

As you wrap up the session, ask students to pair up as accountability partners. Instruct them to share with their partners—

- which of God's attributes is most meaningful to them right now and why
- which of God's attributes is hardest for them to understand or accept right now and why
- how they would explain God's judgments in the book of Revelation to people who don't know much about him

Before you close the session in prayer, ask each student to commit to learning one new truth about God every day for the next week. Encourage students to keep track of their discoveries so they can share them at your next meeting.

The Big Picture:
Limited Perspectives

Skim Revelation 6, 8-9, and 16 then answer the following questions based on what you see there.

1. If all you knew about God was what you read in these four chapters of Revelation, what words would you use to describe him?

2. What would be your personal opinion of him?

3. What would you expect from him?

Read John 3:16, Romans 5:8, and 1 John 4:7-12. Then answer the following questions based on what you find:

1. If all you knew about God was what you read in these verses, what words would you use to describe him?

2. What would be your personal opinion of him?

3. What would you expect from him?

The Big Picture: Match Game

Match the attribute with the definition.

Attributes

_____ 1. Eternal

_____ 2. Holy

_____ 3. Omnipresent

_____ 4. Just

_____ 5. Loving

_____ 6. Omnipotent

_____ 7. Omniscient

_____ 8. Sovereign

_____ 9. Transcendent

_____ 10. Immutable

Definitions

a. God is right here with us—always present, always near.

b. There's never been a time when God didn't exist, and there will never be a time when he doesn't exist.

c. God is perfectly consistent—there's no room for improvement and no chance of decline in him.

d. God can do anything that is within his nature.

e. Everything about God is good and right and perfect—he exists apart from sin.

f. God is the ultimate authority—he answers to no one and is influenced by no one.

g. God isn't contained by the universe or anything in it. He's not subject to the laws of physics or any other constraints in our world.

h. God knows everything that's happened in the past, everything happening in the present, and everything happening in the future—nothing is beyond his understanding.

i. God desires a personal relationship with us and seeks only the ultimate best for our lives.

j. God can't allow wrongdoing to go unpunished—a penalty or punishment must be paid for sin. (Jesus did this for us!)

8

Safe!
Revelation 7; 14

SOUND BITE

While God may allow his people to be touched by hardship and tragedy, he will protect us from being overwhelmed by them.

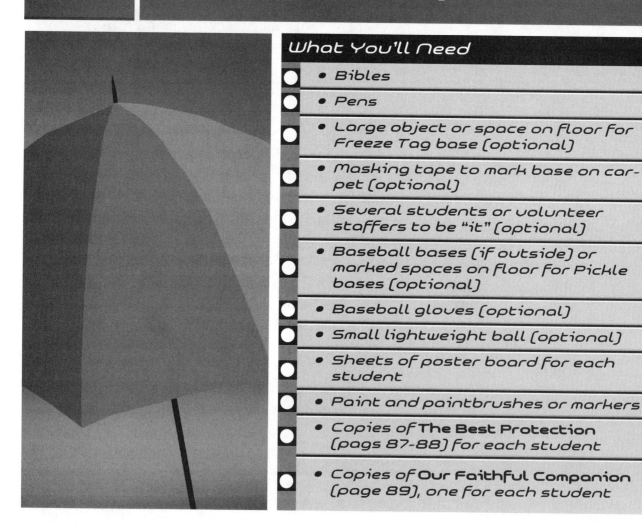

What You'll Need

- Bibles
- Pens
- Large object or space on floor for Freeze Tag base (optional)
- Masking tape to mark base on carpet (optional)
- Several students or volunteer staffers to be "it" (optional)
- Baseball bases (if outside) or marked spaces on floor for Pickle bases (optional)
- Baseball gloves (optional)
- Small lightweight ball (optional)
- Sheets of poster board for each student
- Paint and paintbrushes or markers
- Copies of **The Best Protection** (pags 87-88) for each student
- Copies of **Our Faithful Companion** (page 89), one for each student

You're It (And So Are You!)

Kick off the session with a variation of the old playground favorite Freeze Tag. Before the game secretly inform three or four of your students that they will be it. Explain their goal is to tag as many other players as possible. In order to do that, though, they will need to keep their identity (as it) secret until just the right time in the game.

Announce to the group they will be playing Freeze Tag and that a certain object or location in your meeting area (perhaps marked by tape on the floor) is the base—where players may rest safely—for 30 seconds at a time. No one may be tagged while touching or standing in the base area. After 30 seconds players must move at least 10 steps away from the base before they may return.

Explain when players are tagged, they must freeze (stand still) until they're unfrozen (touched) by another player. Then start the game—without revealing who's it. Leave it to the students you selected before the game to reveal themselves in their own time and in their own way. If you do this right, you can create all kinds of tension and paranoia—first as players wait for the person who's it to reveal himself and again when it turns out there's more than one.

Continue the game until most or all of the players are frozen. Pay special attention to what happens around the base. Afterward introduce the session topic using some or all of the following questions:

YOUTH WORKER SCRIPT

- **How many of you felt safe or confident you wouldn't be tagged when you started the game? Why?**
- **How many of you were surprised by what happened during the game?**
- **What was the best strategy for staying safe during the game?**
- **What's the best strategy for staying safe in everyday life?**
- **In our game the safety feature—the base—was imperfect because you could only stay there a short time. What are some of the drawbacks or weaknesses of your places of safety and security in real life?**

Rundown

Here's another playground game, commonly known as Pickle. Your students will play three at a time. Two players will stand near bases set 20-30 feet apart; the third will start in the middle, between the bases. The game is played like a rundown in baseball (hence the name). The runner in the middle tries to get to one of the bases while the other two players try to tag her with the ball by throwing it back and forth as they close in on her. For the complete effect you could equip your two basemen with baseball gloves.

You may then use the following questions to introduce the topic of safety and security:

YOUTH WORKER SCRIPT

- **In our game the bases were safe. Where do you go for safety and security in your everyday life?**
- **What are some of the things preventing you from finding the safety and security you're looking for?**

Focusing In

Safety First

Distribute large sheets of posterboard and paint or colored markers. Ask students to paint, draw, or otherwise visually represent the safest place they can imagine. Don't give them any more information than that. Let them come up with their own ideas of what it means to be safe. If students are self-conscious about their artistic ability, assure them stick figures and crude diagrams are perfectly acceptable. Afterward ask volunteers to display and explain their work.

You may want to use the following questions to guide your discussion of the activity:

- **How safe is the world you live in?** (If you have students from different backgrounds, encourage them to compare outlooks and explain why they feel as they do.)
- **What are some things that make the world safe?** (To get your students thinking, you might suggest things like seat belts, airbags, police officers, pedestrian crosswalks, and anything else you can think of.)
- **What are some things that make the world unsafe?**
- **What's the most dangerous situation you've ever experienced? How did you escape?** (Encourage volunteers to share, but don't force anyone to relive a traumatic experience.)
- **Do you believe the world is a more dangerous place for Christians than it is for non-Christians? Why or why not?**

MORE MORE MORE

Safety First

The *Safety First* discussion practically screams for dramatic testimony. Invite some friends, acquaintances, or fellow church members who have experienced God's protection in amazing ways to briefly share their stories with your students.

Hitting the Book

The Best Protection

Distribute pens and copies of **The Best Protection** (pages 87-88) to your students while they're in the large group…then let 'em work in small groups to complete the sheet. Also, please gauge how much time you think this worksheet will take your group—feel free to highlight only key questions while eliminating others. You may want to use the following comments to supplement your discussion of Revelation 7 and 14:

- God's judgment, as described in the book of Revelation, is very specific and purposeful. He doesn't haphazardly hurl natural disasters from heaven, trying to hurt as many people as possible. His judgments accomplish exactly what he wants them to accomplish.

- Even in the midst of unprecedented disaster and destruction, God demonstrates his concern and protection for his people. This is an illustration of the truth that God's love exists in perfect harmony with his holiness and justice. One attribute never cancels out or interferes with another, regardless of the circumstances.

- God expects his people to faithfully endure the circumstances we face, no matter how difficult or painful they may be. Along with that expectation, though, God offers himself as a resource for comfort, encouragement, and protection.

- For Christians, faithful endurance of earthly suffering is rewarded by heavenly blessings—not the least of which is the privilege of spending eternity in the presence of God himself.

LET'S GET THEOLOGICAL

The Best Protection

If you want to deal with the *who*, *what*, and *when* of Revelation 7 and 14, point out some Christians believe the "144,000 from all the tribes of Israel" represents the faithful Jews who will be alive during the Tribulation. Other people believe the number represents all faithful believers who will be alive during the Tribulation—in other words they believe the church is "spiritual Israel." Still others believe the number refers to Jewish believers in the past who remained faithful during times of persecution.

You may want to refer to **Judgment Days Defined** (pages 70-71) from session 6 if students need help keeping straight terms such as *Tribulation* (page 71) in session 6 if students need help keeping terms straight.

Making It Count

Our Faithful Companion

Distribute pencils and copies of **Our Faithful Companion** (page 89). Let students work individually, in pairs, or in small groups to complete the sheet—whatever works best for the size of your group. Ask volunteers to share their responses.

As you wrap up the session, you might want to put these questions to your students:

A few more notes about suffering:

- Encourage your students to offer their personal feelings, as opposed to Sunday school answers.
- Supplement their responses by pointing out *why* God allows us to experience tragedy and difficult times—and that even knowing this isn't nearly as important as understanding *how* to respond to such circumstances.
- Instead of causing us to question God's existence or his love for us, our suffering should draw us closer to God and cause us to seek his strength and comfort.
- As many Bible characters discovered, suffering actually serves to strengthen faith. Just as completing a tough workout at the gym builds muscles, working through a tough time in your life in a way that honors God builds spiritual strength and endurance.
- When we've experienced suffering ourselves, we can better empathize with other people who are suffering. When we have firsthand knowledge of the emotions and questions other people are experiencing, we can address them in ways that may make a difference in those people's lives.
- But ultimately we must accept the fact that we will never completely understand or come to terms with God's reasons for allowing suffering. At some point we must accept the fact that he knows what he's doing and trust him to see us through. We must also

recognize no matter how intense things get here on earth, it's temporary. Our eternity is guaranteed to be problem free as we enjoy the rewards of life in heaven with God.

• Close the session with a group prayer. Ask a volunteer to read God's promise in Joshua 1:5: "I will never leave you nor forsake you." Encourage your students to respond to that promise in their prayers—if not aloud then silently—by thanking God for his faithfulness and asking him to help them apply that promise to their lives when they face struggles, persecution, and tragedy.

MORE MORE MORE

Our Faithful Companion

Challenge your students to memorize the passages on **Our Faithful Companion** (page 89). Award prizes at your next meeting to those who can recite the verses with no more than a few minor mistakes. If you want to add some fun to the assignment, announce that in the coming week, you will randomly call each of your students at home; those who answer the phone by reciting one of the verses—instead of saying "hello"—will win fabulous prizes.

WORTHY OF WORSHIP

In a Loud Voice

Chapters 7 and 14 contain vivid examples of worship, Revelation-style! In chapter 7, here's the scene John paints: "After this I looked and there before me was a great multitude that no one could count, from every nation, tribe, people and language, standing before the throne and in front of the Lamb. They were wearing white robes and were holding palm branches in their hands. And they cried out in a loud voice: 'Salvation belongs to our God, who sits on the throne, and to the Lamb.' All the angels were standing around the throne and around the elders and the four living creatures. They fell down on their faces before the throne and worshiped God, saying: 'Amen! Praise and glory and wisdom and thanks and honor and power and strength be to our God for ever and ever. Amen!'" (verses 9 through 12).

In chapter 14, an angel speaks in a loud voice: "Fear God and give him glory, because the hour of his judgment has come. Worship him who made the heavens, the earth, the sea and the springs of water" (verse 7).

Take some time as a group to sing in loud voices to God, giving him thanks for his strength, for his wisdom, and for salvation through Jesus.

The Best Protection

The following questions are brought to you through the courtesy of your leader. The favor of a reply—several of them, actually—is requested.

Revelation 7:1-8

1. The four winds in this passage represent destructive forces of God. Why are they being held back?

2. Why is the seal of God significant in this passage?

3. Can you think of another example in the Bible in which God kept one or more of his people safe despite threatening situations?

4. Do you consider yourself *marked* by God? If so, what does that mean to you?

Revelation 7:9-17

5. What do you notice about the crowd standing in front of God's throne?

6. What makes God the owner of our salvation?

7. How is God's gift of salvation a form of protection?

8. How would you express your praise to God for his gift of salvation?

9. What do you think of the trade off described in verses 15 through 17: *an eternity of service before God's throne in exchange for our hunger, thirst, sadness, and discomfort taken care of forever?*

Revelation 14:1-5

10. In the Old Testament a "new song" celebrated a new experience of God's deliverance or blessing. What does the new song in this passage celebrate?

11. If you were to write a new song about what Jesus has done for you, what would be the title?

12. How are the "144,000" described in this passage?

Revelation 14:6-13

13. What does it mean to fear God? What does it mean to give him glory? What does it mean to worship him?

14. What does the future hold for people who choose to turn their backs on God?

15. In light of the third angel's warning, why would anyone choose to turn her back on God?

16. What is patient endurance (verse 12)? How can a Christian develop it? Why is it important for Christians to develop it?

17. What are some things that make patient endurance difficult?

18. How is the warning in verse 13 similar to the old saying, "Sometimes it's harder to live for Christ than to die for him"? Do you agree? Why or why not?

19. Under what circumstances might it be easier to die for Christ than to live for him?

Revelation 14:14-20

20. What do the images of sickles and harvest suggest to you?

21. Who's doing the harvesting?

Our Faithful Companion

For each of the following passages, replace the crossed-out phrases with words that make the passage more personal to you. For example in Psalm 139:8 you might replace "If I go up to the heavens" with "If I go to college a thousand miles away."

"For I am convinced that neither death nor life, neither ~~angels~~ nor ~~demons~~, neither the present nor the future, nor any powers, neither ~~height~~ nor ~~depth~~, nor anything else in all creation, will be able to separate us from the love of God that is in Christ Jesus our Lord" (Romans 8:38-39).

"Where can I go from your Spirit? Where can I flee from your presence? If I go ~~up to the heavens~~, you are there; if I ~~make my bed in the depths~~, you are there. If I ~~rise on the wings of the dawn~~, if I ~~settle on the far side of the sea~~, even there your hand will guide me, your right hand will hold me fast" (Psalm 139:7-10).

"And surely I am with you always, [even] ~~to the very end of the age~~" (Matthew 28:20).

9

Will This Be on the Test?
Revelation 11-13; 17-18

SOUND BITE

Certain passages of God's Word are difficult to understand—at first glance. Fortunately for us God rewards all diligent, genuine efforts to discover the truth in his Word.

What You'll Need

- Bibles
- Pens
- At least half a dozen treasure-hunt clues hidden at various locations on sheets of paper (optional)
- Transportation for treasure hunt teams (optional)
- Several exciting prizes to award the winning team (optional)
- Snacks hidden in a special place for your students (optional)
- Copies of your coded message for each student (optional)
- Copies of **Say What?** (pages 98-100), one for each student
- Copies of **Good to Know** (page 101), one for each student

Find That Treasure

Before the meeting you'll need to create, prepare, and hide clues for a treasure hunt. You can make the clues as elaborate or as simple as you desire. For example you might—

- Write down a column of numbers that, when added together, reveal a telephone number to call for the next clue.
- Write down the license plate number of a car in the parking lot with the next clue written on its windshield.
- Hand out a photograph of a recognizable landmark where the next clue is located.

Whatever clues you choose to use, you need to make sure each one leads logically to the next one. In other words don't make the clues so obscure your teams can't figure them out. You might also want to set up a clue hotline—using an adult volunteer and a cell phone—for teams to call if they were to get lost or stuck on a clue.

Depending on how much time (and transportation) you have, your treasure-hunting area may be as small as the building in which you meet or as large as your entire city. If appropriate, name the hunt after the item being sought. For example you might hide a man's hat and call your hunt "The Quest for the Brown Derby."

When students arrive for the meeting, divide them into treasure-hunting teams. Distribute the first clue to each team, and let the hunt begin. Award fabulous prizes to the team who finds the treasure first.

Afterward introduce the session topic by explaining you're going to be talking about a different kind of treasure hunt—the search for truth which sometimes seems buried in hard-to-understand Bible passages.

Code Breakers

In place of food on your snack table, put down a stack of papers with the same coded sentence written on each. Explain that the coded sentence reveals where the snacks are located. When students decipher the code and understand the sentence, they can head for the snacks. (Talk about incentive!) Let your students work in pairs or teams to break the code.

There are any number of codes you can use. For example you might substitute each consonant with the letter three consonants after it in the alphabet (so *K* would be written as *N,* and *X* would be written as *B)* and each vowel with the vowel immediately preceding it in the alphabet (so *O* would be written as *I,* and *A* would be written as *Y).*

Here's a sample message you might use:

> THE SNACKS ARE HIDDEN UNDER THE SPARE
> TIRE IN THE TRUNK OF MY CAR.

Translated into the code we just described, it would read—

> XLA WRYGNW YVA LEHHAR ORHAV XLA WSYVA
> XEVA ER XLA XVORN IJ QU GYV.

Segue into the session topic by asking students to think of some other things that sometimes seem to be written in code. If no one mentions them, suggest things like math homework, the fine print at the bottom of a sweepstakes entry form, or the ingredients on a cereal box. Point out that certain hard-to-understand Bible passages may also seem like they're written in code.

Focusing In

Obscure References

Start your discussion by asking the students to explain the meaning of an *inside* joke.
If students don't recognize the term, explain that inside jokes are words, phrases, nicknames, and obscure references only a select group of people understand and appreciate. In other words inside jokes make people say, "I guess you had to be there."

Share with your students a couple of inside jokes or obscure references you and your friends enjoy. Explain—to the best of your ability—what the origin of the joke or reference is, why you and your friends adopted it for personal use, and how it has evolved over the years. Ask volunteers to share some of their own inside jokes and obscure references—emphasizing, of course, that they should be appropriate for the group.

You may want to use the following questions to guide your discussion:

- Have you ever read a Bible passage which seemed like an inside joke to you—an obscure reference only certain people would be able to understand? If so, give us an example.
- How do you respond to or deal with challenging passages in the Bible? Why?
- Why do you suppose God chose to make his Word—or at least parts of it—so challenging to understand? (You'll address this question later in the session. At this point you're just looking for your students' opinions.)

Be prepared to lead by example here and talk about a Bible passage that's always seemed a little mysterious to you or caused you some frustration as you tried to understand it. Talk about how you dealt with that confusion or responded to your frustration at the time.

Segue into the Bible study by pointing out that the passages you're going to be looking at—Revelation 11-13 and 17-18—rank right up there with the most difficult-to-understand passages in all of Scripture.

MORE
MORE
MORE

Obscure References

Explain that Jesus himself often used parables—illustrative stories and examples—to communicate his truths, much to the frustration of his disciples. To give your students an example of what Jesus' disciples were up against, read a couple of Jesus' parables in—

- *Matthew 13:31-32*
- *Matthew 22:1-14*
- *Luke 5:37-38*

Point out that the meanings of Jesus' parables weren't immediately obvious, even to his closest friends. They required a certain amount of thought on the part of his listeners.

Say What?

Distribute pens and copies of **Say What?** (pages 98-100) to your students while they're in the large group…then let 'em work in small groups to complete the sheet. Also, please gauge how much time you think this worksheet will take your group—feel free to highlight only key questions while eliminating others.

Divide the group into three or four study teams. Assign each team one or two sections of the sheet to complete. Ask a volunteer from each team to summarize the team's passages and responses for the rest of the group.

Keep in mind this passage is rough sledding. Make yourself available to answer students' questions, as needed. (In fact you may want to bone up on these passages yourself—and perhaps even discuss them with a mentor—so you'll be ready to address at least some of the questions that come your way.)

You may want to use the following comments to supplement your discussion of Revelation 11-13 and 17-18:

YOUTH WORKER SCRIPT

- **Sometimes remaining faithful to God's call comes at a great personal cost. For the two witnesses (or the countless witnesses symbolized by the two witnesses, depending on your interpretation), remaining faithful to God cost them their lives. In the whole scheme of things, however, that momentary sacrifice pales in comparison to the eternal rewards God has in store for the faithful.**

- **No situation is ever beyond God's power. You'd think the death of the two witnesses would have been the end of their testimony. Wrong. God simply intervened in the physical laws of life and death, in order to accomplish his will. If he can do that, he can certainly intervene in any situation that seems hopeless to us.**

- **God has allowed Satan to have certain controls in our world right now. That means if we're living the kind of life God calls us to, we should expect not only to stand out, but also to be taunted and perhaps even persecuted for our faith.** (And remember, there are governments around the world that persecute millions of Christians under their rule. Check out Student Underground from www.YouthSpecialties.com for more details!)

- Though Satan will ultimately be defeated by God, he's still a powerful force to be reckoned with. Christians shouldn't fear Satan, but we should respect his power and be on our guard against him at all times.

- God will ultimately repay all evil—including the evil directed toward his people—in his time. His judgment will be devastating, complete, and perfect.

LET'S GET THEOLOGICAL

Say What?

Depending on how much exposure you want your students to have to the various interpretations of Revelation 11-13 and 17-18, you could use any or all of the following information:

- Some Christians believe the two witnesses described in Revelation 11 are symbols of believers who share their faith, despite persecution, during the last days before Jesus' return. Other Christians believe the witnesses are actual individuals who will be killed because of their testimony.

- Some Christians believe the Beast (or Antichrist) is a symbolic way of referring to the Roman Empire, and most of the prophecies concerning the Beast have already been fulfilled. Other Christians believe the Beast is an actual person. In fact many famous people throughout history have been accused of being the Antichrist.

- Some Christians believe the Second Beast (or False Prophet) is a symbolic way of referring to religious figures or institutions that actually serve worldly authorities. Other Christians believe the Second Beast is an actual person.

Making It Count

Good to Know

Give your students a chance to vent any frustrations they have regarding the passage they just studied. Then pose the same question you asked earlier about why God would make his Word—at least parts of it anyway—so challenging to understand.

To help answer the question, ask a volunteer to read Matthew 22:37-38. Help your students understand that using our minds—especially in relation to God's Word—is a way for us to show our love and worship for God; it's part of our service to him. The more effort we put into understanding God's Word, the more we honor him.

Ask volunteers to read the following passages:

- *Psalm 119:97-104*
- *Proverbs 2:1-5*
- *Matthew 7:7-8*

You may want to explain that—

YOUTH WORKER SCRIPT

Words such as *search, meditate,* and *seek* make it clear that studying the Bible isn't an activity we should approach casually or passively. If we're going to make sense of God's Word—if we're going to understand what he wants us to understand in it—we've got to bring everything we've got to the table.

That means we can't dismiss the hard parts. If a passage doesn't make sense to us, we need to take whatever steps are necessary to figure out what it means. Here are some ideas to get you started.

Distribute copies of **Good to Know** (page 101). Give students a chance to read through the sheet and ask any questions they have. You may want to use the following questions to guide your discussion of the sheet:

- Which of these hints is your biggest priority right now? Why?
- Who would make a good Bible study mentor for you? Why?
- What effect does regular, meaningful Bible study have on your life? Explain.

Ask a volunteer to read Matthew 7:7-8 again. Point out that God always rewards sincere efforts to understand his Word. In other words if we knock long enough, he will open the door of understanding for us.

As you wrap up the session, challenge each of your students to study—not just read—at least one Bible passage they have never explored in detail before. Encourage them to use the tips listed in **Good to Know,** as needed.

Say What?

Okay, big challenge here! These questions will test you on many levels—and getting to the bottom of them will be tons of fun. But first you need to spend some time with the passages they're based on—and it may get messy! Are you up for this???

Revelation 11:1-14

1. Based on a 30-day month, how many months is 1,260 days?

2. Why is that number of months significant? (*Hint:* Think about the Tribulation.)

3. What do the witnesses' powers and abilities tell you about them?

4. What common ground do you see between this passage and the story of Elijah and the messengers of Ahaziah in 2 Kings 1:10-12?

5. What does the fact that the Beast, or Antichrist, comes up from the Abyss suggest about him?

6. Why do you suppose the world responds so coldly to the witnesses' deaths?

7. Who are God's witnesses today? How do people respond to them?

8. What's the most extreme example of evangelism you've ever seen—or been responsible for?

9. How will the world respond to the sudden resurrection of the two witnesses (verse 11)?

Revelation 11:15-19

10. What do the 24 elders worship God for in this passage? Why is that significant to them?

11. Who will God reward?

12. What is God's reward for those who remain faithful and obedient to him?

13. How do we reverence God's name?

14. What symbols of God's power are mentioned in verse 19?

Revelation 12:1-13:1

15. How would you interpret and explain Revelation 12:1-6 if the woman represents Israel, the dragon represents Satan, the baby represents the Messiah, the desert represents a place of spiritual refuge, and the 1,260 days represent a time of spiritual protection in the face of worldwide persecution?

16. What does Michael's heavenly battle against Satan tell us about Satan's strength?

17. How does Satan lead the world astray?

18. How does the blood of the Lamb overcome Satan?

19. As Christians, what should be our attitude toward Satan?

Revelation 13:1-10

20. Based on the description in this passage, how do you picture the Beast or the Antichrist?

21. How would you interpret verse 1 if horns represent power?

22. How does the Beast get the world's attention?

23. How do you explain his miraculous healing?

24. Why is it important to understand the Beast is *given* his power?

25. Why are people so quick to follow dynamic, compelling leaders?

26. Why are patient endurance and faithfulness important attributes for all Christians?

Revelation 13:11-18

27. What's the job description of the Second Beast (or False Prophet)?

28. What's the miracle—performed by the Second Beast—that gets the world's attention?

29. How will people respond to the image described in verse 15?

30. What's the purpose of the mark described in verses 16 and 17?

31. What will happen to those who receive the mark? What will happen to those who refuse it?

32. Theologians have been trying to figure out the significance of the number *666* for centuries. What's your guess?

Revelation 17:1-18

33. The great prostitute represents Babylon, a satanic civilization notorious for idolatry and sexual sin. Why do you suppose the Beast is so closely associated with such a place?

34. What evidence of idolatry and sexual sin do you see in our society today?

35. What does the Beast do with the power and authority given to him by the kings of the earth?

36. What difference does it make in your life to know that Christ's chosen and faithful followers will overcome the forces of evil?

37. What eventually happens to the great prostitute Babylon?

Revelation 18:1-24

38. How would you sum up the charges against Babylon in one sentence of 10 words or less?

39. What do you suppose inspired Babylon to make such a boastful claim in verse 7?

40. Why is Babylon's judgment so terrifying to the kings of the earth?

41. Why will the saints, apostles, and prophets rejoice over Babylon's fall?

Good to Know

If you're serious about understanding God's Word, you'll need to equip yourself. Here are six quick tips for doing that:

1. Find a translation you can understand.

If you can't understand what your Bible says, you need to find one that makes sense to you. Check out your local Christian bookstore—it'll feature entire aisles of various Bible translations. Take them for test drives until you find one you're comfortable with!

2. Invest in a study Bible.

Whatever translation you decide on, make sure it comes in a study Bible format—most of the major Bible translations do. Among other things study Bibles offer—

- *Individual book introductions that explain when the book was written, who wrote it, who the book was written to, what was happening while it was being written, what's in it, and how it's related to other books*
- *Notes in the margins and in other spots that provide helpful information about individual verses*
- *Directions to other verses dealing with the topic you're studying*

3. Explore other tools.

If you're serious about discovering the wisdom in God's Word, you should make sure your Bible study toolbox is well stocked. Here are some tools you might need:

- **A journal**—*for writing down your thoughts and feelings about what you learn*
- **A Bible dictionary**—*for discovering the precise meanings of scriptural words and phrases*
- **A Bible concordance**—*for linking the passage you're studying with other related passages and for finding relevant passages based on key words*
- **A Bible atlas**—*for locating the sites of various biblical events*
- **A Bible commentary**—*for insight and analysis from biblical scholars*

4. Find a trusted advisor.

If you know a mature Christian whose opinion and judgment you trust, recruit him as a consultant for your Bible study. If you were to find yourself faced with a passage you couldn't understand, talk to him about it—get his input.

5. Pray before you read.

Ask God to clear your mind of distractions when you read and to give you the wisdom to interpret his Word as he intends it to be interpreted.

6. Get it in your head!

The more time you spend in God's Word, the more comfortable you'll become with it. As different passages become familiar to you, you'll begin to spot connections and inside information that will help you understand them better. So read it as much as you can!

10

The Final Showdown
Revelation 19-20

SOUND BITE

Though it may seem that evildoers prosper all around us, the time is coming when evil will be defeated once and for all—that's when it will pay big-time to be on God's side.

What You'll Need

- Bibles
- Pens
- Several short team games (and required equipment) from different genres—an athletic game, an intellectual game, an artistic game, etc. (optional)
- Several fun or silly prizes to award the winners of the various games (optional)
- Sheets of poster board for each group of students (optional)
- Scissors and glue or tape for each group of students (optional)
- Several old magazines and newspapers for each group of students (optional)
- Copies of **One Way or Another** (pages 110-111) for each student
- Copies of **Payback** (pages 112-113), one for each student

Choose Up

Announce that you're going to divide the group into two teams for a competition. But don't tell your students what the competition is. Ask one or two of your most athletic students—without pointing them out as such—to move to one side of the room to form the nucleus of the first team. Ask one or two of your brainiest students to move to the other side of the room to form the nucleus of the second team. Then have the rest of the students choose which team they want to be on. Emphasize that the relative size of the teams doesn't matter. If 99 percent of your students want to join one team, that's fine.

If most of your students choose to align themselves with the athletes, make the competition a trivia contest or Bible knowledge quiz. If most of your students align themselves with the brainy team—as unlikely as that may seem—make the competition a relay race or some other athletic event. If the teams are pretty equally split, make the competition a neutral event, such as building a house of cards. As a reward for choosing the right team, distribute prizes to the winning players.

Keep in mind the competition isn't as important as the choosing of teams. Pay close attention to the things students say and do as they make their team choice. Refer to their comments and actions when you debrief the activity.

Segue into the lesson with questions like—

YOUTH WORKER SCRIPT

- Why did you choose the team you chose?
- If you'd have known what you know now, would you have made the same team choice? Why or why not?
- In what ways is being a Christian like being on a team?
- Why did you make the choice to join the Christian team?
- Do you ever think about what it would be like to be on the other team, spiritually speaking? Explain.

Collage Education

Divide students into pairs or small groups. Distribute posterboard, scissors, tape or glue, and a stack of old magazines and newspapers to each group. Ask students to make a collage—a collection of pictures and words clipped from the periodicals and positioned together on the board—titled "Evil Is…"

Don't define the word *evil* in this context. Encourage students to base their collages on their own standards—or, better yet, their understanding of *God's* standards—of good and evil. Afterward give the groups a chance to display and explain their collages. If you get some differences of opinion as to whether certain things are evil, encourage a little friendly debate among your students.

Discuss the collage project with questions like—

YOUTH WORKER SCRIPT

- **What is evil? How would you define it?**
- **What makes people choose to do things that go against God's will?**

If no one else mentions it, suggest that people sometimes choose to go against God's will for profit or personal gain. Many people have no problems ignoring God's will or disobeying his laws if doing so will help them get ahead or satisfy an immediate desire.

Finally segue into the session topic by saying something like—

YOUTH WORKER SCRIPT

You might say people who do evil for their own profit or personal gain are on a different team in life than those who try to do things for God's glory and God's gain. As Christians we're on God's team.

Focusing In

One Way or Another

Use any or all of the following questions to kick off your discussion:

YOUTH WORKER SCRIPT

- How do you feel about being a member of God's team?
- Most teams have rules and restrictions their members must abide by. What are some of our rules and restrictions as members of God's team?
- Will people who aren't bound by God's laws have an advantage in our society? Explain. (If no one mentions it, remind students of corporate scandals in which people made millions of dollars by lying, cheating, and stealing. Remind them, too, of so-called bad boy and bad girl celebrities who get rich and famous by pushing the boundaries of decency and morality.)
- Which is easier—being a member of God's team or being a free agent who lives according to his own rules, does whatever he needs to do in order to get ahead, and seeks only to satisfy his own desires? Explain.

Distribute copies of **One Way or Another** (pages 110-111). Let students work in pairs or small groups to complete the sheet. You may want to use the following questions to guide your discussion the sheet:

YOUTH WORKER SCRIPT

- Which of these situations would present the most temptation for you? Why?
- Have you ever faced a similar experience?

Ask volunteers to describe a situation in which they could have benefited from ignoring God's Word or his will for their life. Be prepared to lead by example and share one of your own experiences. Talk about how you could have benefited, how tempted you were to disobey "team rules," and what the consequences (both good and bad) were of your decision.

One Way or Another

Instead of having pairs or small groups *write* their responses, ask volunteers to act them out. Give your volunteers time to come up with two brief role plays for each situation—one demonstrating the easy solution (and potential consequences) and one demonstrating the tougher, God-honoring solution (and potential consequences). After each presentation discuss as a group the implications and results of each option.

Hitting the Book

Payback

Distribute pens and copies of **Payback** (pages 112-113) to your students while they're in the large group...then let 'em work in small groups to complete the sheet. Also, please gauge how much time you think this worksheet will take your group—feel free to highlight only key questions while eliminating others. You may want to use the following comments to supplement your discussion of Revelation 19-20:

YOUTH WORKER SCRIPT

- God is perfect in every way, and we definitely fall short of God's standards with every breath we take.
- Anyone who takes the Bible seriously must recognize that choosing to disobey God is never a wise decision—no matter how much it may benefit us in the short term—because the ultimate price is just too high.
- The fact that God is the ultimate Judge, and he won't allow evil to go unpunished, should inspire worship in us, as it does in the creatures of heaven.
- Any rebellion against God, whether it takes place in a person's heart or on a battlefield with millions of soldiers, will end badly for the person or persons in rebellion.

- Though Satan is described in Scripture as the ruler of this world, he's ultimately subject to God's control. When God deems it necessary to have Satan disappear for a millennium, he sends an angel to toss him into the Abyss. When God determines Satan's time is over for good, he throws him into the lake of burning sulfur.
- God rewards those who believe in him. One of those rewards is the right to reign with Christ.

LET'S GET THEOLOGICAL

Payback

You may want to use the following information as needed to introduce students to the eschatological aspects of this passage:

- Some Christians—known as *premillennialists*—believe Satan will be bound when Christ returns at a future time. They believe the 1,000 years referred to in Revelation 20 is a literal period when Jesus will rule with his people on earth—specifically in Jerusalem. They believe the Millennium will conclude with Satan being freed from the Abyss. They believe the Millennium will be followed by the Great White Throne Judgment and then the creation of the new heaven and new earth.
- Some Christians—known as *amillennialists*—believe the binding of Satan represents Jesus' victory at the cross. They believe the millennium represents the Church Age in which we're currently living. They believe Satan will be turned loose for a brief period at the end of the age to wreak havoc until Christ returns. They believe the dead will be resurrected and good and evil will be judged at Christ's return.
- Some Christians—known as *postmillennialists*—believe essentially what amillennialists believe, except for the fact that they believe the Church's spreading of the gospel will eventually reduce Satan's influence in the world to virtually nothing, thus binding him.

Making It Count

A Foregone Conclusion

To drive home the point of the session, you may want to put the following scenario to your students:

YOUTH WORKER SCRIPT

What would you do if you were to open the sports page tomorrow morning and see a play-by-play account—and a final score—of a game that won't be played until next week? Think about it. What if you could know for sure which team would win and exactly how the game would turn out?

Let students weigh in on their reactions to such foreknowledge. If no one else mentions it, suggest that for many people, the logical response would be to withdraw a large sum of money, head for Vegas, and bet everything on the winning team.

Continue with something like—

YOUTH WORKER SCRIPT

When you think about it, this passage in Revelation 19-20 is like a news report from the future. Thanks to God's revelation to John, we know how the battle of good versus evil is going to end. We may not be able to break the bank in Vegas with that knowledge, but we can benefit from it.

First of all we can make sure we're on the right team. Choosing good over evil isn't always an easy decision—especially since people who choose the wrong path often seem to get further ahead, gain more popularity, and enjoy themselves more than we do. In other words in the battle between good and evil, evil seems to be winning the early rounds. But since we know how the fight ends, we can stay faithful to God's will and his plans for us—no matter what other people do.

Secondly we can get actively involved in the battle. We can take a bold stand for God and his will. In some cases that will involve making the right personal decision at the right time. In other cases it may involve taking an unpopular position on a controversial issue. In other cases it might mean going against the crowd—or even against your own friends.

Give students a chance to pair up with accountability partners. Instruct them to think of one way they can show their team colors in the coming week by taking a bold stand for God at school, at work, or at home. Encourage accountability partners to share their ideas with each other and then brainstorm specific strategies for making those ideas work.

Close the session in prayer, asking God to bless your students' efforts to take a stand for him and to use their boldness to further his glory.

MORE MORE MORE

A Foregone Conclusion

If you'd prefer a more hands-on activity to end the session, try an art project, letting students work in pairs or small groups. Distribute art supplies and paper to each group and instruct students to design and create posters—or for those who are artistically challenged, come up with bumper sticker slogans—communicating in a creative, memorable way the truth that evil will ultimately be defeated.

WORTHY OF WORSHIP

Keeping Our Eyes on the Ball

Chapter 19 contains a great example of misplaced worship: "Then the angel said to me, 'Write: "Blessed are those who are invited to the wedding supper of the Lamb!"' And he added, 'These are the true words of God.' At this I fell at his feet to worship him. But he said to me, 'Do not do it! I am a fellow servant with you and with your brothers who hold to the testimony of Jesus. Worship God! For the testimony of Jesus is the spirit of prophecy'" (verses 9 and 10).

Invite students to share about times where they were drawn to worship something other than God. Discuss why we're so drawn to temporal things—everything other than our one, true heart's desire. Sing a song of worship to God that emphasizes how worthy he is to be praised!

One Way or Another

For each of the following situations, come up with an easy solution (one not necessarily taking into account things like right or wrong) as well as a tougher solution (one that would be expected from a member of God's team). Also think about the consequences—both good and bad—of each solution.

Situation 1

In your locker you find an embarrassing picture of the person who stole your boyfriend or girlfriend. Obviously the picture is a gift from an anonymous friend who wants to see you do something humiliating—and public—with it.

Easy Solution
The easy solution would be to...

The good thing about choosing that option would be...

The bad thing about choosing that option would be...

Tougher Solution
The tougher solution would be to...

The good thing about choosing that option would be...

The bad thing about choosing that option would be...

Situation 2

Your best friend was part of a group that broke into the school Saturday night and trashed a couple of classrooms to the tune of about $2,500 in damage. The only reason you know about it is your best friend called to tell you how scared he is about getting caught. Just before the end of the day on Monday, the vice principal calls you to her office, where a police officer is waiting. The officer asks you if you know anything about the incident on Saturday night.

Easy Solution

The easy solution would be to...

The good thing about choosing that option would be...

The bad thing about choosing that option would be...

Tougher Solution

The tougher solution would be to...

The good thing about choosing that option would be...

The bad thing about choosing that option would be...

Situation 3

You're getting the cold shoulder from everyone at your new job in the local music store. When you ask the assistant manager about it, she tells you candidly she and the other employees have a "help yourself" attitude to the merchandise. They each take a couple of CDs a month—enough to make working at the store worthwhile, but not enough to arouse the manager's suspicions. She tells you the other employees are afraid you'll blow the whistle on them and ruin their little on-the-side venture.

Easy Solution

The easy solution would be to...

The good thing about choosing that option would be...

The bad thing about choosing that option would be...

Tougher Solution

The tougher solution would be to...

The good thing about choosing that option would be...

The bad thing about choosing that option would be...

Payback

Be a sport, and read the following passages and then answer the questions that go with them, 'kay?

Revelation 19:1-10

1. Why should we praise God for his judgments?

2. What does it mean that God's judgments are true and just?

3. What does God avenge in his punishment of Babylon, "the great prostitute" (verse 2)?

4. What does it mean to fear God (verse 5)?

Revelation 19:11-21

5. Who's the rider described in this passage? How do you know?

6. How do the armies of the earth react to the coming of the rider?

7. Describe how you picture the eternal fate of the Beast and the False Prophet.

8. What does the battle described in this passage tell us about God's judgment?

Revelation 20:1-6

9. What's the purpose of locking up Satan for 1,000 years?

10. Describe how you picture life on earth during Satan's absence.

11. Who's given the authority to judge during the Millennium?

12. Why are those who are part of the first resurrection called blessed?

Revelation 20:7-10

13. What happens when the 1,000-year period is up?

14. Who does Satan recruit for his last stand against God?

15. How does Satan's story end?

16. Describe how you picture existence in the lake of burning sulfur.

What It All Comes Down To
Revelation 20

11

SOUND BITE

One day everybody will be judged by God. Those who aren't saved by faith in Christ will be separated from God forever. As Christians that should be major motivation to share the Good News of Jesus with as many people as possible.

What You'll Need

- Bibles
- Pens
- Materials like old tires or boxes for an obstacle course (optional)
- Blindfolds for each pair of students (optional)
- Stopwatch (optional)
- Several exciting prizes to award the winners of your obstacle course (optional)
- Flip chart or whiteboard and pens (optional)
- Blindfold for each Speed Pictionary team (optional)
- As many Speed Pictionary words as there are students (optional)
- Copies of **The Verdict** (page 121), one for each student
- Copies of **The Strategy** (pages 122-123), one for each student

Kickoff Option ❶

A Little Help

Set up an obstacle course in or around your meeting area. You can make the course as simple (using just the chairs in your room) or as elaborate (using tires, wading pools, balance beams, and anything else you can think of) as you wish. Divide the group into pairs, and explain that one member of each pair will be blindfolded. That person will attempt to navigate the obstacle course based on the verbal instructions of the other partner.

Emphasize that partners may not have any physical contact at all during the contest. Success will be determined by how well the sighted partner gives guidance and how well the blindfolded partner follows instructions. Award prizes to the pair who successfully navigate the maze in the shortest amount of time. If you have time let partners switch roles and try the course again.

Segue into the session topic using questions like—

YOUTH WORKER SCRIPT

- **How hard was it for those of you who were blindfolded to follow your partner's instructions? Explain. What could they have done to be more helpful to you?**
- **For those of you who did the guiding, what was the secret to successfully leading your partner through the course? If you were to do it over again, what would you do differently? Why?**
- **Give some examples from everyday life of people benefiting from the guidance or instructions of other people (e.g., learning how to drive, learning how to multiply, learning how to spell, learning how to ride a bike, etc.)**

If no one else mentions it, point out that unbelievers benefit from having the Good News of God's love and Christ's sacrifice explained to them by caring Christians. We are called to guide them to salvation.

Kickoff Option ❷

Speed Pictionary

Divide the group into two or more teams for a contest that will challenge their drawing skills, among other things. Make sure that each team has its own flip chart or white board, marker, and blindfold.

Here's the way the game will work: When you say, "Go," the first artist on each team will run to you to get a clue, run back to the group, put on a blindfold, and try to draw the clue for the rest of the team to guess. When the clue is guessed, the next person on the team runs to you for a clue and repeats the process. Be sure you have enough words for everyone on the team. The team to guess all of its words first wins.

Afterward you may want to use the following questions to debrief the activity:

YOUTH WORKER SCRIPT

- **How easy was it for you to guess the clues that were being drawn? What would have made it easier?**
- **Why is drawing while blindfolded such a challenge?**
- **Have you ever had an experience when you felt you were being led or taught by someone who didn't know what he was doing—like someone wearing a blindfold?**

To segue into the session topic, you may want to say something like—

YOUTH WORKER SCRIPT

As Christians we don't have to worry about drawing blindfolded in life. Thanks to God's Word, we can see the whole picture of our future. That makes us valuable to the people around us, whether they realize it or not. Many of them are so desperate for information about the future they're willing to turn to fortunetellers and false religions for answers. That's why it's important that we share what we know, based on our unobstructed view.

Focusing In

Personal Testimony

Spend some time discussing your students' personal testimonies and the details of how they came to a saving faith in Christ. Be sensitive to the possibility that not all of your students have made personal commitments to Christ. Use any or all of the following questions to guide your discussion:

- Who led you to Christ?
- What did the person say or do that got your attention and made you want to hear more?
- Was there anything going on in your life making you especially receptive to the Good News of Jesus? If so, what? How did it affect you?
- What specifically did you do when you made the decision to accept God's gift of salvation and make Jesus Lord of your life?
- How did you feel after you accepted Christ? Did you notice a change in your life right away? Explain.

Be prepared to answer each of these questions yourself to give your students an idea of the kind of responses you're looking for. Don't force anyone to share, but encourage your students to offer as many details as they're comfortable with.

Continue your discussion with questions like—

YOUTH WORKER SCRIPT

- What happens when people place their faith in Christ?
- Do you believe you have a responsibility to talk to other people about Christ? Explain.
- How can you use your personal experience of being led to Christ in your own witnessing efforts? What can you learn from the person who was most instrumental in leading you to Christ? What mistakes would you like to avoid?
- Do you ever feel a sense of urgency about sharing your faith with other people? Why or why not?

MORE MORE MORE

Personal Testimony

If you have students who enjoy performing, recruit them to role-play scenarios illustrating the right way and the wrong way for a Christian to witness to an unbeliever in certain situations. Encourage them to use humor in their presentations, but to keep the scenarios fairly true to life.

Hitting the Book

The Verdict

Distribute pens and copies of **The Verdict** (page 121) to your students while they're in the large group…then let 'em work in small groups to complete the sheet. Also, please gauge how much time you think this worksheet will take your group—feel free to highlight only key questions while eliminating others. You may want to use the following comments to supplement your discussion of Revelation 20:

YOUTH WORKER SCRIPT

- **No one is exempt from appearing before God's judgment seat.**
- **Because nothing is hidden from God, everything—from our most obvious actions to our most secret thoughts—will be exposed and examined on the day of judgment.**
- **Only those people who are saved by their faith in Christ will escape judgment. Therefore, there's no reason for Christians to fear God's judgment—at least not for ourselves.**
- **The Great White Throne Judgment isn't where God decides who'll go to heaven and who'll go to hell. It's more like the official pronouncement of guilt and the sentencing phase of the trial. Those who refuse to accept God's free gift of salvation are condemned the moment they die.**
- **Scripture suggests there will be degrees of punishment in the lake of fire. Everyone there will suffer, but some will suffer more, based on their earthly actions.**
- **Elsewhere in Scripture the word everlasting is used to describe the punishment of those whose names aren't found in the Book of Life (2 Thessalonians 1:5-10). There's no indication in the Bible that God will ever put people out of their misery—so to speak—and simply do away with the lake of fire and everyone in it. Instead their torment will last forever.**

The Verdict

Invite a leader from your church who's knowledgeable about (or good at) evangelism ministry to talk briefly to your students about the nuts and bolts of sharing the gospel. Contact your students before the meeting and encourage them to prepare some questions about witnessing they can ask your guest speaker.

Making It Count

The Strategy

Ask your students how the judgment scene in Revelation affects their motivation or commitment to sharing their faith with others. Then ask them to talk about whether the desire to prevent their loved ones from facing the Great White Throne Judgment ever figures into their thinking when it comes to sharing their faith.

Distribute copies of **The Strategy** (pages 122-123). Give students a few minutes to complete the sheet. When they're finished pair them up with accountability partners to discuss what they wrote. Encourage your students to open up to their partners and share their strategies—as well as their hopes and fears—regarding witnessing to the people they singled out.

To enhance the interaction throw out one or more of the following questions for accountability partners to discuss regarding the people listed on their sheets:

YOUTH WORKER SCRIPT

- **How aware is this person of your Christian faith? What does this person think of your faith?**
- **Have you ever had conversations about spiritual topics with this person before? If so, how did they go?**
- **On a scale of one to 10—with one being totally uninterested and 10 being totally interested—how interested might this person be to hear what you have to say about your faith?**

Close the session by asking accountability partners to pray together about the important faith-sharing opportunities ahead of them in the coming week. Encourage partners to contact each other periodically throughout the week to check on how things are going.

MORE
MORE
MORE

The Strategy

To assist your students in their faith-sharing efforts, plan an outreach event for your entire group. Whether you make it a game night, a movie night, a food night, or something else, your first priority should be to plan an event your students would feel comfortable bringing their non-Christian friends to. Sometime during the meeting you—or one of your students—should make a few brief comments to the group, explaining what your youth group is all about and briefly explaining the spiritual bonds tying you together.

The Verdict

Do we really need to tell ya to read the Bible passage below and answer the questions that follow? Didn't think so!

Revelation 20:11-15

1. Who is seated on the Great White Throne?

2. What does the fact that the earth and sky flee tell you about what's coming?

3. Who are the defendants at the Great White Throne Judgment?

4. Describe the scene before God's throne, as you picture it.

5. On what basis are the dead judged?

6. What happens to those people whose names aren't found in the Book of Life?

7. Describe how you picture the lake of fire.

8. What does a person have to do in order to deserve punishment in the lake of fire?

9. If you could explain this passage to unsaved friends or family members, would it make a difference in their attitude toward Christ and Christianity? Why or why not?

10. How do people get their names written in the Book of Life?

The Strategy

1. In the space below write the name—or if you prefer the person remain anonymous, the initials—of someone you know and care about who isn't a Christian.

2. If you were to ask why this person isn't a Christian, what kind of response would you receive? Check any of the following reasons the person might give—or add your own.

   ❏ *I don't know anything about Christianity.*

   ❏ *I'm not a religious person.*

   ❏ *I think Christians are hypocrites.*

   ❏ *I'm having too much fun right now.*

   ❏ *I think it's narrow-minded to believe one religion is better than another.*

   ❏ *I've done too many bad things in my life.*

   ❏ *I'm a good person—that's all that matters.*

   ❏ *I think Christianity is a crutch for people who can't deal with real life.*

   ❏ *I have my own personal reasons for not wanting to have anything to do with God.*

   ❏ Other: _____

   ❏ Other: _____

3. How would you reply?

4. What would be the best way to start a conversation about Jesus with the person?

5. What specific points would you want to make? (Don't forget to include Bible verses you'd like to share.)

6. What might happen—good or bad—if you were to actually share your faith with the person?

7. Do you believe the potential results are worth the risk? Why or why not?

12

To Infinity and Beyond
Revelation 21-22

SOUND BITE

As Christians we're guaranteed eternal happiness, joy, and fulfillment in God's presence. And though we may not know exactly what our eternal home will be like, we can rest assured it will surpass even our wildest expectations.

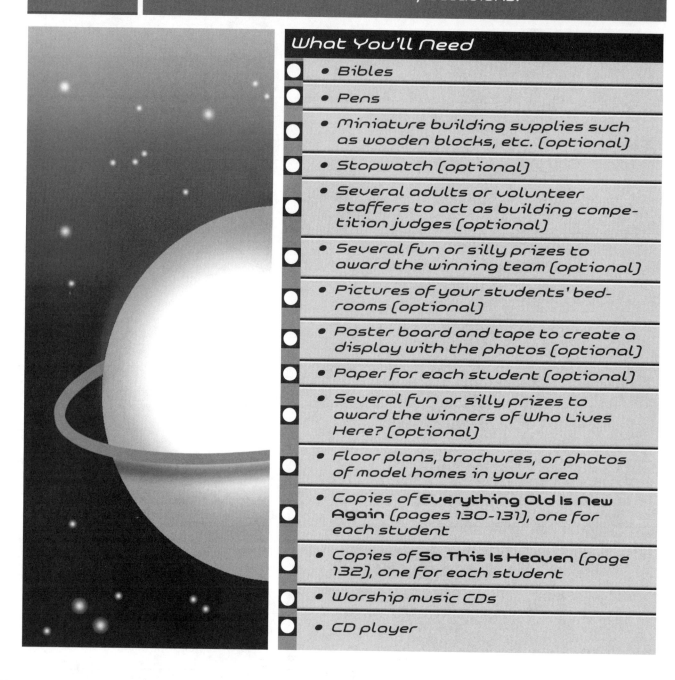

What You'll Need

- ○ • Bibles
- ○ • Pens
- ○ • Miniature building supplies such as wooden blocks, etc. (optional)
- ○ • Stopwatch (optional)
- ○ • Several adults or volunteer staffers to act as building competition judges (optional)
- ○ • Several fun or silly prizes to award the winning team (optional)
- ○ • Pictures of your students' bedrooms (optional)
- ○ • Poster board and tape to create a display with the photos (optional)
- ○ • Paper for each student (optional)
- ○ • Several fun or silly prizes to award the winners of Who Lives Here? (optional)
- ○ • Floor plans, brochures, or photos of model homes in your area
- ○ • Copies of Everything Old Is New Again (pages 130-131), one for each student
- ○ • Copies of So This Is Heaven (page 132), one for each student
- ○ • Worship music CDs
- ○ • CD player

If You Build It...

Divide the group into teams. Give each team an equal supply of wooden blocks or any other toy building supplies you can get your hands on. Set a time limit (10 minutes or so) for each team to build the best possible structure it can. When time is up bring in an unbiased panel of experts—or anyone you can round up on short notice—to judge the structures based on their size, aesthetics, and sturdiness. Then declare a winner and award prizes to the winning team.

Segue into the lesson by saying something like—

YOUTH WORKER SCRIPT

The effort you put into these buildings has given you a small glimpse into the tremendous amount of planning and effort that goes into constructing an actual home.

**MORE
MORE
MORE**

If You Build It...

Instead of using judges to settle the issue of which house is best, use tennis balls. Distribute tennis balls to each team and let players take turns trying to knock down each other's structures—from a competitive distance of course. The team with the last structure standing is the winner.

Kickoff Option   2

Who Lives Here?

Before the meeting you'll need to take a picture of each student's bedroom. You can do this in one of two ways: You can give your students advance warning and allow them a chance to clean their rooms first—the polite-yet-boring option—or you can get permission from your students' parents to do a surprise shoot, showing up unexpectedly to photograph the bedrooms in all their disgusting glory—the embarrassing-yet-interesting option.

Display the photographs on a large piece of posterboard, with a number next to each one. Distribute paper and pens and ask students to try to match each bedroom with the person it belongs to. Award prizes to the person with the most correct answers.

Segue into the session topic using questions like—

- What does your bedroom—your personal living space—say about you?
- If you were to change three things about your bedroom, what changes would you make? Why?

Focusing In

Cribs

Before the meeting you'll need to collect floor plans, brochures, or photos of several different model homes in your area. If you can find material for mansions and estates—as well as typical middleclass homes—this activity will work much better.

Display or distribute the material to your students. Instruct them to mentally mix and match aspects of different houses to create their dream homes. Encourage students to dream big and assume money is no object. Then ask volunteers to describe to the group their dream homes in as much detail as possible.

Continue the exercise by asking volunteers *where* they would like to live: an urban, a suburban, a mountain, a rural, an ocean setting—or even in a different country. Or anywhere! Ask them to paint a verbal picture of their future dream home.

Then segue into the session topic by asking students how they picture their eternal home—the place they'll live forever and ever. Encourage several students to offer their descriptions of heaven.

Then ask a volunteer to read John 14:1-3. You may want to use the following questions to supplement your discussion of the verse:

YOUTH WORKER SCRIPT

- What kind of a place might Jesus be preparing for each of his followers?
- How does this promise of Jesus make you feel? Why?

You may want to point out in the New King James Version *rooms* is translated as *mansions*. In other words our heavenly dwelling is something to be excited about!

Wrap up this section by pointing out that you're going to be looking at the passage in Scripture revealing more about what heaven is like than any other in the Bible—the last two chapters of Revelation.

Cribs
Here's another line of housing-related questions you might want to pursue with your students:

YOUTH WORKER SCRIPT

- If you were to choose your neighbors for your ideal house—the people you want living closest to you—who would you choose? **Why?**

- What about your heavenly neighbors? **Who would you like to spend eternity with in heaven?**

- What steps have you taken to make sure those people will be in heaven with you?

Hitting the Book

Everything Old Is New Again

Distribute pens and copies of **Everything Old Is New Again** (pages 130-131) to your students while they're in the large group…then let 'em work in small groups to complete the sheet. Also, please gauge how much time you think this worksheet will take your group—feel free to highlight only key questions while eliminating others. You may want to use the following comments to supplement your discussion of Revelation 21-22:

YOUTH WORKER SCRIPT

- Heaven is the eternal reward for all believers. That's not to say any of us has earned the right to go to heaven, though; our salvation is an undeserved gift from God.

- The apostle John's description of heaven may be difficult to fully comprehend, but it does give us a sense of heaven's awesome splendor. Think about it—walls and gates made of precious stones; streets made of pure, transparent gold; a river flowing from God's throne; brilliant brightness coming from God himself. What could be more incredible?

- God is the source of all happiness, joy, and fulfillment—the closer we get to him, the happier, more joyful, and more fulfilled we are. In heaven we will be in the presence of God, which means we will experience perfect happiness, joy, and fulfilment…forever.

- The awesome beauty of heaven and the presence of God himself will trigger our eternal attitude of worship and praise. Faced with our surroundings we won't be able to keep ourselves from worshiping God.

- If you've ever considered the idea of worshiping God for all eternity as boring, try this on for size: Imagine you're in the audience of the greatest rock concert of all time—minus crowd problems and even the security guards who line the stage to keep you away from the Star of the show. This time you're invited on stage and sing a few verses with everybody cheering. Now…multiply that by a million. And keep that intensity going on and on and on. You never get tired or bored.

That will give you a tiny glimpse of what it might be like to worship God for all eternity!

Making It Count

So This Is Heaven

Distribute copies of **So This Is Heaven** (page 132). Let students work in pairs or small groups to complete the sheet. Use any or all of the following questions to guide your discussion of the sheet:

YOUTH WORKER SCRIPT

- Where do your ideas of what heaven is like come from?
- How accurate do you think your visions of heaven are? Explain.
- What are your overall feelings about eternity? Explain.

Wrap up your session—and this study—with a mini worship service. Focus your praise on the fact that God has made it possible for us to spend eternity with him. Play familiar praise choruses or contemporary Christian songs to set the mood. Ask volunteers to share some of the things they're looking forward to about heaven, then close the service in prayer, asking God to bless your students' desire and commitment to praise and honor him and to help them understand what genuine worship can do for their lives.

WORTHY OF WORSHIP

So This Is Heaven

For an unforgettable worship experience, let your students plan and execute the mini-service themselves. Assign different elements of the service—prayer, Bible reading, personal praise, testimonies, and music—to different individuals or pairs within the group. Those individuals or pairs will then be responsible for either fulfilling those roles themselves or finding someone else to do it. Make sure each student has a vital role in your worship planning and execution.

Everything Old Is New Again

Step 1: Read the assigned passages.

Step 2: Answer the assigned questions.

Step 3: Fold your hands in your lap and wait silently for everyone else to finish.
   (Okay, you can skip Step 3, but we'd really appreciate it if you would complete Steps 1 and 2!)

Revelation 21:1-27

1. What's the first detail the apostle John gives regarding the new earth? How would that change the face of the earth?

2. What does it mean the "dwelling of God is with men" (verse 3)? Why is that significant?

3. How does John describe what life will be like on the new earth (verse 4)?

4. Why does God refer to himself as "the Beginning and the End" (verse 6)?

5. Who will inherit the eternal riches God has in store?

6. What will be the eternal fate of unbelieving people?

7. Based on John's description in verses 11 through 27, how do you picture the Holy City? (Keep in mind "12,000 stadia" is about 1,400 miles.)

8. Why is the temple—a place of worship—unnecessary in the Holy City?

9. Why are the sun and moon unnecessary in the Holy City?

10. Describe what life will be like without any impure, shameful, or deceitful influences to worry about.

Revelation 22:1-21

11. Compare Revelation 22:3 with Genesis 3:1-24. What's the curse we're currently living under?

12. What will life be like when the curse is lifted?

13. Jesus spoke the words, "I'm coming soon!" more than 2,000 years ago. How do you explain that seeming contradiction?

14. What mistake did John make in his excitement over seeing heaven?

15. How did the angel respond?

16. Why does God issue such a strong warning against adding to or taking away from the prophecy he gave?

So This Is Heaven

Based on what you read in Revelation 21-22—as well as your own ideas about what heaven's like—list some things you're looking forward to about eternity and some things you're not so sure about.

I'm looking forward to . . .

I'm not so sure about . . .

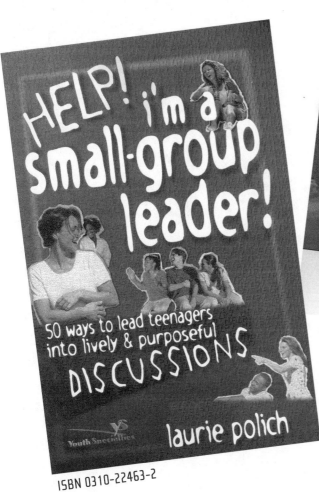

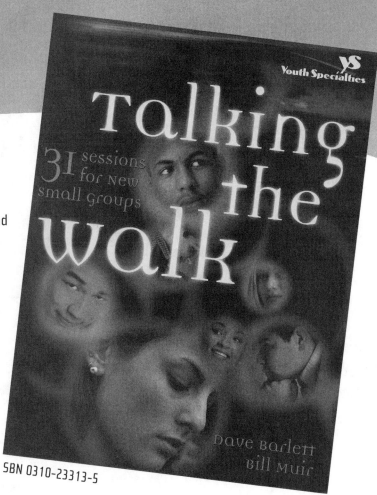